THE SECRET PSYCHOLOGY OF LEARNING ENGLISH

THE SUBCONSCIOUS WAY

SURABHI JAIN

Contents

Contents

Acknowledgements

MESSAGE FROM THE AUTHOR

I am immensely grateful that you have picked up this book, and I wish and genuinely hope that it will serve the purpose with which it was written- to walk you through a journey of transformation towards becoming a natural, confident, and fluent English speaker, following the secret psychology of learning English and the failproof trusted regimented techniques.

This book is ME, as I have lived all the problems and the consequences of being a bad English speaker, mentioned in this book. It is said unless you experience something, you can't write about it. This book is all about why and how I am a Public speaker and a communicator today. The stories, the experiences, the research, and the strategies are a part of the journey towards being a Fluent speaker.

Be it in personal life, in professional life, or be it in social life, we need to be fluent and confident speakers. We all wish to speak English powerfully, quickly, effortlessly, fearlessly, automatically, and naturally, we all envision being successful speakers.

This book Intends to walk you through a transformative journey of being a Fluent speaker through some exciting and practical exercises and practices. I wish and believe that this book will help you take that first step toward becoming an impactful speaker. You have a lot of potential in you, keep exploring yourself and keep practicing.

I express my gratitude to my mother who had only one dream which was to see her daughter speak fluently and confidently just like Mrs. Indira Gandhi. Thanks to my father for being my strength. My heartfelt thanks to my husband for relentlessly motivating and encouraging me to follow my passion for becoming an English trainer. My love to my daughters who have been the supporting pillars in my journey.

And special thanks to my mentors, who inspired and supported me in conceiving the idea and writing this book.

I would like to thank the almighty for blessing me with this beautiful life!

Lots of Love and Gratitude to my beloved readers!! I humbly dedicate this book to all my readers. The world needs more and more confident English speakers, and I wish and hope you become one.

Thank You! Thank You! Thank You!

With lots of Love and Respect,

Surabhi Jain

Prologue

That winter afternoon in 2001, when I was struck by the reality of being hit hard enough to make me sweat at 22 degrees Celsius.

I remember I was in the meeting room; everyone was pouring out ideas. Bringing their innovative thoughts to the table. Some ideas involved huge expenses, and some demanded huge manpower. The room bubbled with chatters and there was me, just nodding my head in agreement, as though I understood everything.

Suddenly, my boss asked me, "Surabhi, what do you think, will it work?" Suggestions flustered my mind and I was sure I was going to blow everyone with my ideas and yes, I spoke, "I-I-I think I-I-it's a-a good idea". I spoke in English, broken English. The fear of English speaking turned me into a bundle of nerves, causing me to sweat, feel giddy and sink into my chair.

It was evident, that I was suffering from the world's most serious epidemic – **"THE ENGLISH TRAUMA"**

I belonged to a middle-class family, which knew only one language- Hindi. My mother (a big fan of Mrs. Indira Gandhi, the then Prime Minister of India), wanted to see her daughter become a leader & speak fluent English like her. So, I was sent to an English medium school, which essentially meant that all the subjects were taught in English. And soon the classes felt stressful and the tests felt super complicated and it scared me. We were expectedto memorize long lengthywordlists and long answers from notebooks.

The school only reconfirmed my belief- "I always believed English is complicated." I started to lose even the little confidence that I had. I started to believe English was just not my cup of tea, and I had no confidence at all, to speak in English.

Years passed. While I fared well in academics, the fear of communicating in English was still alive in my mind.

soon after I entered college, I realized that I needed to speak fluent English confidently, not only to thrive but even to merelysurvive in this cut-throat competitive world. Speaking in

English was not merely a skill, but a differentiator. It was the necessity of the hour.

I have to speak English. Of course, it was formidable and stressful. While I ardently wished to speak fluent English, the constant humiliation and mockery by peers made me believe that my English-speaking ability was damaged. I understood I can't and would never be able to speak in English.

And as it is said, "You are what you think." I proved myself right. For a long time in my life, I hadno friends, no social life, and no confidence. That's how it was. Life went on this way.

The biggest realization happened when one day, we were visited by my father-in-law's cousin from the US. My father-in-law ushered my daughters to greet him. It was heart-breaking to see my daughters stuttering, shivering, and blushing with embarrassment. Subconsciously, I had spread the infection (the fear of English) to my daughters.

As a mother, this reality hit me hard on the face, and perhaps that was the day of my revelation too. The infection for sure had spread to my daughters.

That day, I made up my mind, "My daughters will not live with the same resentment., NO."

So, I decided to find a cure for this disease. It was because of this disease, I had lived most of my younger days with the tag of a shy hesitant girl. It was this same disease now that was slowly cribbing into my daughter's life. Their personality development was at stake. Because of this disease, my kids' personality was getting devastated.

This is when my journey or rather I would proudly call it- 'My Transformation Journey started. The journey was nowhere close to easy but it is worth every bit of it.

Every class I joined, every course I joined taught me complex grammar rules, expected me to memorize exhaustive vocabulary lists, and put us in conversational roleplays, where we had to speak forcibly, feeling uncomfortable, humiliated, and stupid. With every mistake, we made; we were corrected by the teacher instantly.

Besides, I found it difficult to comprehend when the teacher spoke fast in English. All of these only added to my fears and made me feel more anxious, nervous, and shy, whenever I opened my mouth. I felt embarrassed about my bad pronunciation and once again I was unknowingly going into the shell- The shell that I had created for myself.

I was frustrated with my slow and broken English. I felt miserably hard to understand the instructions of the teacher in English. I started feeling anxious again, and this time more strongly that, felt that I will never master this language in my life. **ENGLISH IS NOT MADE FOR ME.**

This was another defining moment of my life that is worth mentioning. It was then I started working upon not just myself but building a framework for all others who faced the same struggle.

While I was battling with my fears, I also realized that there were many like me who were grappling with this disease, mentally and emotionally. Even after spending years learning the language people are still struggling to speak fearlessly and naturally. People who are scuffling with English Trauma, not only lack the ability to speak fluent English but also undergo resentment, discontent, frustration, and anxiety, all of which hinder their overall personality.

Besides my years of experience, I have also surveyed 200 people who were carefully selected from a varied set of demographics based on certain criteria.

And while the results of the survey appeared to be predictable on the surface, a deep analysis led to some eye-opening results (discussed at length later in the book.)

Here are a few highlights of the survey report:

1. A good number of people mentioned that they are scared of speaking in English.

2. Many people assume that only speaking English makes you sound knowledgeable and smart.

3. Maximum people say that they suffer nervousness and anxiety when they have to speak in English.

It is evident that the traditional English education system is broken. I believe that there must be a better way to learn English, something different from what we had been following blindly.

I began to search for a better way. Then I started to research and study studied a lot about second language learning., I read the theories of various linguists like Dr. Noam Chomsky & Dr. Stephen Krashen. Stephen Krashen, a linguist at the University of Southern California stated: "We acquire language when we understand what people tell us and what we read....... there is no need for deliberate memorization."

If most of us agree that the best way to learn English is naturally, it pains to observe that most of the trainers and teachers, and even the students are inclined to choose the old ineffective, slow, and unnatural ways.

I finally realized that the problem was not with me, the problem was with the old-school traditional teaching methods. These methods are confusing and stressful. They damage the student's ability to speak good English. These methods are complete failures. They make you forget about your real goals, like a successful career and exciting international travels. The ultimate purpose of learning a language is categorical and rigorous communication. They made you believe "English is difficult and you are bad at learning English"

I started doing my informal research. I interviewed many people who have learned and mastered this language only as an adult. I observed certain-fixed patterns. These people were mostly successful adults who mastered English outside school or at a later stage in life. Their methods were quite similar to what I had researched. Most of them avoided the traditional methods used in schools.

So, I started trying & creating some strategies to practice and polish my English-Speaking skills. Gradually, I started training my kids using the same methodologies. My kids began to show improvement. We were able to speak easily and naturally. Most of all, we were enjoying the process. Slowly I involved my friend's kids and it got transformed into a regimented learning Program "Smart

Kid's Grooming Classes."

As of today, while I am writing this book, I havetrained more than 550 students in 7 years. Along with this, I have been constantly improving myself with each passing day.

I underwent the training as an IELTS trainer and also earned my certification as a Business Communication Coach and soft skills trainer. In the following years, I brought home several accoladeslike The Global Teachers Award in 2019, for my contribution to Training space & India's Business Conclave Award, and for being the best English Speaking Training Institute in Lucknow.

The newfound confidence and the accolades added to my passion to go deep into research in this areaAlong with this I did more research and the process, and I discovered the unique unconventional methods that became the basis for my English learning system. This system was the cradle of my flagship program called 'The Turbo English Mastery Program.'

The onset of the Pandemic in 2020 allowed me to connect with people across the nation and beyond. Eventually, the techniques started benefitting college students, teachers, trainers, corporates, and professionals. The "Turbo English Mastery "Program" helped thousands of people to overcome their fear of English speaking, move forward in their journey of English learning, and achieve the goal of fluency. In 2021, I got an opportunity to speak and share my transformation journey on the many prestigious and coveted platforms.

Now, while the story of my transformation might sound inspiring, but probably I know you are also quite skeptical "Whether these methodologies going to work for me too?" Yes, they will work for you.

If you have picked up this book, chances, are you have been trying to become a fluent English speaker for a while. You have invested long hours, studying grammar, cramming exhaustive vocabulary lists, and acting in various roleplays. Chances are you might have attended various lectures, and classes, and followed an end number of courses, YouTube videos, podcast channels, and websites to improve your speaking ability. Undoubtedly you have been trying hard to learn English following the traditional ways.

You must be thinking, "How can I learn English subconsciously without any conscious effort & learning?"

First, let us understand why is English learning so painful?

Let me tell you about my student, Saima, her dream was to work for multinational companies such as Unilever, P&G, Coca-Cola, etc. Sadly, her dream remained unfulfilled because of her broken English speaking ability. Even more intriguing fact was that she had been learning English for over 10 years!

She knew a lot of vocabulary words. Her English grammar was excellent. She could understand, read and write English very well. But after years of learning, she couldn't speak English fluently.

"How do you learn English?" I asked her.

"Well, I learn vocabulary and grammar rules and then try to put them together to make correct sentences. It's That's how I learned English in high school and this is how it's supposed to be, isn't it?" she repliedhesitantly.

I understood why she couldn't speak English fluently even after years of learning. It's because she had learned English in a very UNNATURAL WAY. It's the traditional way which I was following when I started my journey of English speaking. It is the conventional method, almost all of us had been following. You cannot speak English easily by learning individual words and grammar rules and then putting them together. It's not mathematics, where you can apply formulas and derive the answer. And the answer will be either correct or wrong.

Spoken English is a skill, not a subject. There is no wrong or right way of saying things. Your thoughts and ideas can be expressed in a multitude of ways.

Many people make this mistake: They learn individual words and grammar rules and then try to put them together to make a grammatically correct sentence. Just like doing addition or subtraction or performing science experiments.

It's not a NATURAL way to learn English speaking. That's not how children learn a language. That's not how native English speakers learned to speak English. They don't think about grammar rules and focus on applying them to speak accurate English.

Some of my students have more than 5,000 words in their vocabulary bank and are very good at English grammar but cannot speak English well because of this poor learning strategy.

Finally, this book is a solution. The unconventional way to learn English subconsciously and speak naturally and automatically just like the native speakers.

This book is a strategical approach to guide you on your path to fluency. It will help you speed up the journey to becoming a confident and fluent speaker.

In this book, you will learn the correct mindset and psychology to learn English and follow a powerful and effective skill set to help you become a natural English speaker. Additionally, you will also learn how to become a better communicator and use English to grow in your career and achieve the success you dreamt of.

The book is specifically written in the simplest English so that you don't have to sit with a dictionary to read this book.

In the following chapters, I will describe the "Secret Psychology of Learning English" explicitly. You will understand that along with a proven method, the correct psychology is equally important for learning a language. You will learn the step-by-step procedure to use this method and reach the ultimate goal of fluency in English in less than expected time.

In this book you will find illustrations, graphs, diagrams, and tables, along with practical exercises at the end of a few chapters, to facilitate your learning.

Continue reading the book and enjoy the ride. Don't be apprehensive about unlearning your traditional education methods. Get ready to overcome the fear, stress, and boredom. Alter to the most English Learning Classrooms you have been a part of, this journey is going to be filled with fun & enthusiasm.

Have faith in me, I have helped myself and thousands of individuals and professionals and now I am so eager to help you.

Take my words, I will do my utmost to help you become a natural and fluent speaker.

WHAT IS THE SUBCONSCIOUS WAY?

The term 'Subconscious' is used for the uncontrollable or automatic functions of the brain, such as heartbeat, and signals to increase chemical output; which do not require any conscious efforts. It effectively runs the body for you, as well as coordinates learned movements such as riding a bike or driving a car, or playing the piano.

Just think about any other acquired skill you have- driving a car or playing an instrument or anything else that you are quite good at. Do you think about how to switch gears and when to switch from second to third gear while driving? If you would, your car would be jerking as if you drove it for the first time. Do you put conscious effort while playing piano, while pressing those white and black keys? Of course not! You don't or else you couldn't play in the rhythm.

The commonality between the two actions is- **AUTOMATIC ACTION**. If you act automatically, you perform well as your conscious mind is not working.

The truth is that the 'subconscious mind' is responsible for everything that you have in your life. It is the single most powerful part of the human mind. Whatever enters into the mind through a subconscious process will have a better retentiveness. In other words, it will stay longer and could be recalled or retrieved easily.

It is this psychology that is the basis of learning English effectively and naturally, using which you will be able to speak powerfully and automatically, without any conscious effort.

Human beings have been using Language to express their ideas and feelings with the help of signs and symbols. The information inside the brain is encoded and decoded through these signs and symbols. There is a multitude of languages spoken in the world. The mother tongue or the native language is the first language learned by a human as a baby. It is the language, which he or she listens to from his or her birth. Any other language learned or acquired is known as a second language.

For instance, since birth, I have been surrounded by people who spoke Hindi. My parents, family members, neighbors, and everyone around me. So it is my native language or the first Language – FL. I had made no efforts to learn this language and I acquired it. It was an automatic natural process. Whereas, English is a language that I learned when I started going to school and tried to learn it through conscious efforts. So, it is a second language for me. English learning, was the result of direct instructions on grammar rules. It included formal education that helped me learn through more **conscious processes**. (Grammar rules, exceptions to the rules, syntax, vocabulary lists, pronunciations, and so on).

Second language acquisition, or SLA, is the name of the theory of the process by which we acquire - or pick up - a second language. This is primarily a **subconscious** process that follows while we concentrate on effective communication, not on language. **Learners can acquire a language through a subconscious process during which they are unaware of grammatical rules.** Similar to how they acquired their first language. They just repeat whatever is said to them, getting a **feel for what is and what is not correct.** They get the "Sense of Correctness"

Perhaps one of the most significant discoveries made in the recent years, by the researchers in second-language acquisition, is something that most people knew already: acquiring a second language is not simply a matter of 'knowing the rules. Real English fluency is **subconscious knowledge**, similar to knowledge of a first or native language. Fluent speakers, and fluent native language speakers, don't consider grammatical rules when they are speaking or understanding English, in fact, most of the speakers may have never consciously 'learned' the rules they use so well.

(Grammar rules are helpful, yet in certain limited situations: good 'grammar' users can apply conscious rules when they have time to think about and use them, for instance, while writing, but research indicates that grammar usage makes minimal contribution to grammatical accuracy. For most people, forcing 'grammar' in real conversation only causes trouble. Constant reference to rules, makes one's speaking broken and hesitant, which is quite unpleasant to the listener. The moment we get a chance to speak with a fluent English speaker, many of us have the bad habit of constructing our sentences by applying grammar rules, while the other person is talking, which means that we are not listening! And we might end up giving a reply which is not at all related to the context of the conversation. Thus, the essence of communication is lost.

Adding up, learning English the subconscious way is all about finding a state of automatic language usage. It means you don't struggle as you speak. You don't think about grammar rules or translations. You don't feel nervous or stressed. When you learn subconsciously and speak automatically you concentrate and focus only on your ideas. You express your thoughts ideas and suggestions explicitly. Your complete focus is on connecting with people rather than conjugations and vocabulary. And therefore, the process of English speaking becomes an enjoyable experience.

It's time to take a leap of faith and commit yourself to a new system of English learning, following "The Secret Psychology of learning English- The Subconscious Way"

CHAPTER ONE

LOVE IT- ENGLISH IS MADE FOR YOU.

We have accepted and relish Western food, for instance, Chinese, and Italian. We have also adopted western clothing, for example, Jeans, coats- suits, as if they were always a part of our Indian culture itself. Why is it that we are still apprehensive about English speaking? We still feel hesitant, afraid, uncomfortable, and less confident, when it comes to using this language in our day-to-day lives. Why is English still a foreign language for us?

English should not be considered a foreign language. In fact, we should be grateful enough to have the English language in our lives.

Usage of the English language in India is not so new. For this, we need to move a couple of years back and look into our history. The introduction of the English schooling system in India is synonymous with, T.B. Macaulay's Minutes of Indian education, 1835', the common mindset is that English education was a ruse of the Britisher's divide and rule policy and was imposed on the Indians to create a division between the elite and the commoners. Some Indians also believe that this was a plan to crush the ancient Indian education system. But the wheels of this had been set in motion much earlier. The new force was given to education from two sources of a different character.

One was from the Christian missionaries and the other from a "semi-rationalist" movement. The Christian missionaries had started their educational activities as early as 1542, upon the arrival of St. Francis Xavier. Afterward, the movement spread throughout the land and exercised a lasting influence on Indian education. It gave a new direction to elementary education through the introduction of instruction at regular and fixed hours, a broad curriculum, and a clear-cut class system. By printing books in different vernaculars, the missionaries stimulated the development of Indian languages. But hand in hand with the study of the vernaculars went "English education," or the teaching of Western subjects through the medium of English.

In 1817 the semi-rationalists, led by the celebrated reformer Ram Mohun Roy, thought that better things could be achieved through the so-called English education.

Raja Ram Mohan Roy was an Indian religious, social, and educational reformer who challenged traditional Hindu culture and indicated lines of progress for Indian society under British rule. He is sometimes called the father of modern India. As a youth, he traveled widely outside Bengal and mastered several languages—Sanskrit, Persian, Arabic, and English, in addition to his native Bengali and Hindi. In 1805 he was employed by John Digby, a lower company official who introduced him to Western culture and literature. For the next 10 years, Roy drifted in and out of British East India Company service as Digby's assistant.

Originally the British went to India as tradesmen, but gradually they became the rulers of the country. Despite this, the company did not recognize the promotion of education among the people of India as a part of its duty or obligation. It was only in 1813, when the company's charter was renewed, that a clause was inserted requiring the governor-general to devote not less than 100,000 rupees annually to the education of Indians.

When the Bengal government proposed a more traditional Sanskrit college, Roy protested that classical Indian literature would not prepare the youth of Bengal for the demands of modern life. He proposed instead a modern Western curriculum of study. Roy called for the establishment of a college devoted toEuropean learning instead of a Sanskrit college. He questioned the usefulness of Sanskrit studies. He argued that the lakh of rupees devoted to the education of Indians which Parliament had written into the East India Company's charter in 1813 should be laid out in employing European gentlemen of talents and education to instruct the natives of India in mathematics, natural philosophy, chemistry, anatomy, and other useful sciences that have raised them above the inhabitants of the rest of the world.

Here, I would like to mention, The Japanese emperor, who brought Americans into Japan to teach the latest science and literature to the Japanese, in the Meiji revolution (an era of Japanese history that extended from October 23, 1868, to July 30, 1912), so that they could modernize rapidly. The Meiji era was the first half of the Empire of Japan, when the Japanese people moved from being an isolated feudal society at risk of colonization by Western powers to the new paradigm of a modern, industrialized nation-state and emergent great power, influenced by Western scientific, technological, philosophical, political, legal, and aesthetic ideas. As a result of such wholesale adoption of radically different ideas, the changes to Japan were profound and affected its social structure, internal politics, economy, military, and foreign relations

The same sentiment was being expressed by Raja Ram Mohan Roy. Eminently sensible. He believed that English education was more scientific in approach and its introduction in India would help in establishing a more knowledgeable clear and comprehensive system of instruction. He believed that the change in Indian society was possible by routing out mechanical and traditional Sanskrit Shastras. Raja Ram Mohan Roy was not against the study of Sanskrit. He wanted to eliminate mechanical cramming. He was opposed to the Sanskrit method of teaching. He wanted Science instead of scholasticism. Raja Ram Mohan Roy believed in synthesis, synthesis of European Science, and literature with Hindu Shastras or Hindu literature. Though ancient texts such as Vedas and Upanishads and Quran, presented a deep philosophy, he realized that the English education system would teach scientific subjects such as Mathematics Physics Chemistry, and even Botany.

In 1817, he supported David Hare's efforts to find the Hindu College, while Roy's English School, taught Mechanics and Voltaire's philosophy. In 1825, he established Vedanta college, where courses in both Indian learning and western social and physical sciences, were offered.

On one hand, it was convenient and cheaper for the British to use English as a language of instruction instead of trying to translate all their books into local languages, on the other hand, it allowed, over the next 150 years, many Indians to appreciate the development of liberty in England and elsewhere, and to understand advances in science. He was very much influenced by the liberal thinking of the British and as well as by the radical thinking of France.

Almost 12 years after, Roy's idea of English education in India, became an official policy, and the foundation of the kind of 'New India' was laid. In 1835 Lord William Bentinck, the then Governor-General of the British East India Company passed the legislative Act of the council of India- the English Education Act 1835. Under this act, financial support was given to the establishments teaching a western curriculum, with English as the medium of instruction. Measures were taken to promote English as the language of administration and the higher law Courts. This made English one of the languages of India, rather than simply the native language of its foreign rulers.

YEAR	DEVELOPMENT
1542	The Christian missionaries had started their educational activities upon the arrival of St. Francis Xavier.
1813	The company's charter was renewed, and a clause was inserted to devote not less than 100,000 rupees annually to the education of Indians.
1813	Raja Ram Mohan Roy argued for employing European gentlemen of talents and education to instruct the natives of India.
1817	the semi rationalist movement was led by Ram Mohan Roy, for English education.
1825	Ram Mohan Roy established Vedanta college, where courses in both Indian learning and western social and physical sciences, were offered.
1835	Lord William Bentinck, passed the legislative Act of the council of India- the English Education Act 1835.

Yearwise Development of English Language in India

Although confined to a few, English education produced memorable results. It not only qualified Indians for taking their share in the administration of their country, but it also inspired them with those liberal ideas which were sweeping over England.

This understanding of the advances in political philosophy and science ultimately gave us our 1950 liberal constitution which has so far held India together and enabled us to become a (relatively speaking) powerhouse in science and technology. Without the disciplined governance and common language (English) introduced in India by the British, India would have been a splintered sub-continent with over 100 "nations", today, something like Africa. Thus, taking India from an anarchy in the early 18th century to a strong world power of the 21st century, India was Old World, despotic, and truly backward in thinking. The storm of freedom was aroused in India through books and education, not through British rule. That is what ultimately matters, not who rules. When it dawns on people that they rule themselves, no one except themselves can rule.

The purpose of making English a part of your life, accepting it as your language and not as a foreign language, is to prepare ourselves to engage in a society that is becoming increasingly internationally oriented. Today Raja Ram Mohan Roy's philosophy of English education is very significant. Today for free and open access to universal knowledge and a free share of thoughts with the rest of the communities of the world, the language required is English. According to the BBC News article published in 2012, India claims to be the world's second-largest English-speaking country. The estimate is around 10% of its population or 125 million people. Today more Indians speak English. Today with respect to English, the popularity of Sanskrit and Persian, and Arabic is at a lower limit. Don't you think we should be grateful to the English language for making our lives simpler, easier, liberal, and free?

Let us not consider it a foreign language or the second language. As the celebrated author Chetan Bhagat, puts across in his book, "What young India wants"- **Hindi is our mother, English is wife, and it is possible to love both.** Let us love it and speak it just the way we speak our mother tongue or native language. Let's not learn it, let us acquire it like our native language. Let us not just study it, let us use it as we know it, fearlessly, effortlessly, automatically.

CHAPTER TWO

WHAT'S WRONG? - THE DRAWBACKS OF THE TRADITIONAL ENGLISH TEACHING SYSTEM

My efforts to learn English and studying at various institutes, following a multitude of online and offline courses under several mentors and failures, made me realize one thing- "Something is wrong with the English Education System". Every person I met during my journey of learning, as well as training, was dealing with the same situation. They were living with stress & anxiety, boredom, and frustration.

Few of my students had been learning English since childhood. Even I belonged to an English medium school which means I was being made to learn English from the age of 4 years. Yet we failed to speak fluently and confidently.

But we are not alone. This is moreover a Global problem. I call this blend of failure and pressure, the "English Trauma".

One of my students Anugya, a psychologist by profession, hated to speak in English. Learning English for her was a tedious exhaustive and boring task. She shared, "The first time when I was in the classroom, where the instructor was teaching in English and the classmates were also speaking in English, I got a panic attack. How am I going to survive in this atmosphere?" Every time she had to speak in English with her patients or colleagues, she instantly felt hesitant and jittery. Several times she broke into tears due to the humiliation and frustration she had to face because of her inability to learn & speak English adequately. She realized she was undergoing this psychological problem called English Trauma.

I met so many people and it was so heart-wrenching, people were fighting with this mental condition, a severe injury, a deep wound. They were the people who believed English learning was essential for them, they wanted to learn it but they did not enjoy the process. Most of them suffered from the same resentment and frustration as Anugya did.

The more people I met, the more I was inclined to find the cure to this disease, this trauma. Just recall, when you visit a doctor for any kind of ailment, before recommending you the treatment, the first thing the doctor does is diagnose the problem. To diagnose any disease, we need to understand the root cause of the problem. So, what was the cause of the suffering, misery, and failure of the English learners? Even after putting in long years of study, hard work, and patience, why are they unable to speak English fluently and fearlessly?

Is there something wrong with them or is it with the education system itself?

1. Grammar-Translation method

Almost every English-speaking class I joined, focused on teaching obscure grammar rules and of course not forgetting the exceptions to the rules. And we were supposed to memorize all those rules, for tests. This memorization did help me to clear the various tests with good scores. I could read and write well. But did that help me to speak well?

I remember, one day one of my colleagues, Reena asked me, "What are your plans for this vacation?" As I opened my mouth to speak, I thought, "My holidays are planned, so it's confirmed that I will go. So, I must use 'will' and 'the verb in the future tense', so I should say "I will go to Goa, next month".

Oh, wait! I am just about to go next month, so I should use the present progressive tense. So, I must say "I am going to Goa next month" Analysis of complicated grammar rules made my speaking slow and broken. The time it took, to process all those rules and vocabulary words when listening or speaking at a normal speed made me feel frustrated with my English.

Confusing

There are millions of English learners who think of such questions. The moment they come across a new sentence, they try to understand, "how some words and groups are being used in that sentence? Which Grammar tense is being used in the given sentence? So on and so forth. The reason is that we are taught to think about English in terms of grammar only.

Most of the time when students call me or come to me for English improvement, they say they want to improve their grammar. When I ask why? The answer is "because I want to start from scratch." Is it? Does Grammar study form a strong base for English? Let us understand.

Only for reading and academics

In the Western world, "Foreign" language learning in schools was inseparable from the learning of Latin or Greek. As different languages began to be taught in educational institutions in the eighteenth and nineteenth hundred centuries, the Classical Method (Grammar-Translation) was embraced as the central means for teaching foreign languages. Little idea was given to showing oral utilization of languages. All things considered, languages were not being taught essentially to learn oral/aural communication but to learn for being "academic" or, in certain cases, for acquiring a reading capability in a foreign language.

Grammar- Translation was born of German scholarship, the object of which, (as quoted by Kelly 1969) according to one of the critics, W H.D Rouse, was “to know everything about something rather than the thing itself”

And that is what we are doing for decades. We are more concerned with knowing, and studying the English language rather than using the language itself.

Brown H.D. (1994), in his Principles of Language Learning and Teaching, states “It (Grammar) does virtually nothing to enhance a student’s communicative ability in the language.”

Serious & complex

The schools and traditional English teachers favor the Grammar-translation method because it seems to be more academic and serious in approach. Following textbooks, lectures, notes, and memorization.

The method although is a complete failure. It doesn’t help the students to become fluent and natural speakers. The irony is that despite the failure, the teachers moreover the learners prefer to continue to follow this method.

2. Communication Approach

Due to the incompetency and failures of the Grammar- translation method the schools and colleges came up with a communicative approach, wherein they added a clot of communication activities to their curriculum. Activities like:

- Group discussions
- Meeting

- Dialogues
- Public speaking
- Speech
- Sketch or drama
- Storytelling

These activities involve

- Dividing students into pairs or groups
- Reading or repeating dialogues from the textbooks
- Answering questions from worksheets

Unreal

Are these activities anywhere near to the real-life English conversation? Imagine you come across a person with whom you have to converse in English, will he refer to a Q&A worksheet to talk to you or will you refer to a textbook to reply to his questions.

Ineffective in real life

As per research made by Shih-Chuan Chang Department of Foreign Languages, in consistency with Xu Yingcai (1991), language has a vast range of syntactic and lexical info in addition to such a lot of practical and notional possibilities that obviously no second language learner is capable of covering them all in his or her study. This is especially true in the case of the students trained under the communicative- approach because they're bound to specific sentence structures. Many times, they might be required to express what they've never come up with during the course of their learning. In this situation, they are compelled to create something on their own. As they lack the expertise in real-life communication, they're in all likelihood to make wrong sentences.

As a result, the communicative approach is as ineffective as the Grammar Translation Method. It is quite evident that these are not working. But the teachers won't accept, moreover the students won't accept.

3. Passive learning

One major problem with Traditional English Teaching is that it makes English learning a passive activity. Many English students as a foreign language (EFL) college students who are searching for admittance to a college in which English is the medium of instruction do not have sufficient language abilities to recognize lectures, understand textbooks, participate in class discussions, or generate satisfactory written work. In many instances, they have simply experienced teacher-centered instructions, where they have been passive learners. They just

- Sit on chairs in the classrooms,
- Listen to the teacher delivering the lecture
- They make notes
- Merely memorize the notes so collected.
- Appear for a test.

Clearly, learning English is a passive activity.

Speaking is not a passive activity.

Speaking a language, be it English or any other language cannot be a passive activity. You have to communicate with real people spontaneously. You need to interact actively. You have to indulge in a series of questions and answers. Moreover, you need to be ready for the unexpected because the conversation is not planned it may take any course.

Cause of silence

The most critical question is which causes the silence from students: the survey carried out in these studies exhibits that the students do not dare to speak so much in elegance, to show their admiration to the instructor. In addition, earlier than completing the training, the instructor typically asks college students: "Are there any questions?

"The answer in the refrain is "no".

But the teacher must not feel satisfied and understand this as the "entire understanding" of college students because

1. they honestly are aware of that,
2. they do not have anything unclear or
3. they do not know how to ask,
4. they do not know what to ask, and
5. they do not know anything to base on to think further, as well.

With these problems, the time has come whilst the solution for English Classes needs to be rediscovered, to alternate from "sleepy" to "exciting" and "interesting" atmosphere.

Low energy

Passive learning makes English low energy activity. In traditional language learning classrooms, the students are glued to their chairs for a long period. The longer they sit, the lower their energy drops. Concentration and focus are directly proportional to the energy. There are 3 types of learners, Visual, Auditory, and Kinaesthetic. Confining to chairs drains their energy making the body inactive leading to an inactive mind.

The truth is all humans are kinaesthetic learners to some extent. A survey was conducted by the English Education Program, Faculty of Cultural Studies, Universitas Brawijaya

This study investigated the primary Learning style of 3rd-semester college students of the English Language Education Program in the Faculty of Cultural Studies at Universitas Brawijaya in keeping with gender. The sample of the research comprised a hundred students- 34 male students and 66 girl students. All contributors were administered an Indonesian-translated version of Reid's (1984) Perceptual Learning Style Preference Questionnaire consisting of Visual, Auditory, Kinaesthetic, Tactile, Group, and Individual including 30 items.

The result indicated that the foremost male's learning style was kinaesthetic and an estimated 14 male students (41%) while female students turn out to be kinaesthetic and Group and the percentage was the same, 21 students (332%) for kinaesthetic and 21 (32%) students for the group. The results indicate that both males and females tend to be kinaesthetic.

So, the language learning process should be energetic and kinaesthetic.

4. *Fixed Answers*

One of the major drawbacks of Traditional English Teaching is the Fixed answer mindset. The textbook study makes the students believe that there is only one right answer, one right way to communicate in a particular situation.

For example, they may teach you certain fixed ways of salutation, greetings, or farewell. They may tell that stories are always told in the past tense. Why?

English Language or any Language is an ocean of words, phrases, idioms, and slangs. There are multiple ways of saying the same thing. We can change the verb tense to change the emotions behind the story. We can use different vocabulary and phrases. Why can't I tell the story in the present tense? One should be aware of all the permissible answers to a question for example an answer to the question- 'Where are you going tomorrow?' could be - I'm going to the library, or 'To the library' or simply 'Library'. All are correct.

This may confuse the typical English learners. They may get upset with the thought of telling the story in the present tense. The reason is that they have been hardwired to believe that there is only "One Correct Answer"

Or for instance, you need to talk about the day's weather. Can you follow a fixed pattern? The weather is changeable, so should be your answers.

What happens when people want to talk in a friendly relaxed way? The result is very different from what textbooks about English conversation usually lead one to expect, both in subject matter and construction. And, for the English learners who find themselves a part of such informal situations, there are immediate problems of comprehension and oral fluency.

We CAN break the grammar rules at times. Fixed Answer Mentality is limiting as well as confusing. It makes the students rigid, less creative, and unimaginative. Whereas real-life conversations require flexibility and dynamic spontaneity.

5. Fear of Making Mistakes

I remember I was standing in front of the class. when I started speaking, the entire class was listening. All the 48 eyeballs were gazing at me. Feeling the panic and stress, I began to speak, "Today morning the first thing I do.......". "DO? it will be DID." Instantly the teacher corrected me. That was super embarrassing. It made me feel stupid. And the other students who were listening, dare not attempt to undergo such embarrassment.

Two large-scale surveys were conducted at the University of Hong Kong, the surveys indicate that most students have enjoyed inadequate speaking opportunities at school, where "listening to the teacher" has been their most frequent classroom experience. Many students show low confidence in their ability to speak impromptu, they feel unease when speaking it. There are two reasons to increase this unease-

- students' anxiety to speak well
- some teachers' error treatment techniques.

The fear of making mistakes is directly related to the "Fixed Answer mindset". This is indeed the most negative outcome of Traditional Teaching Methods. How is this training imparted to the students? Through quizzes, tests, and exams. The students are supposed to answer the questions asked by the teachers and that answer is the fixed- correct answer. In the absence of that answer, the students are given punishment in the form of poor marks scores or grades.

Students instantly get wired to think that mistakes are not good and must be avoided. They start avoiding anything which is different from the teacher's expected answer. Furthermore, they don't attempt to speak in front of groups or the class because of self-doubt. It's obvious, as they are in the process of learning they will commit a few mistakes. When the teacher corrects the mistakes, they get super embarrassed and feel humiliated.

Error correction

By training them to avoid mistakes and correcting errors the teachers are training them to avoid anything in which they can't be perfect. Here we need to understand, that there is nothing as perfection when it comes to English speaking. Even the native speakers make mistakes- wrong grammar, faulty pronunciation, forgetting vocabulary words. The reason is their main focus is on communication not on language or scores.

The truth is you will make multiple mistakes in your journey to fluency. But don't be disheartened. The natives or other English are least bothered about your mistakes. All they are concerned about is your brilliant ideas, amazing suggestions, exclusive thoughts, and wonderful stories. They want to connect and communicate with you as a human being, not a robot who is fed to speak a limited number of words and sentences. So just forget about perfection and be a natural communicator.

6. Few more reasons

The paper of English Language and Literature Studies; Vol. 2, 2012, Published by the Canadian Center of Science and Education states that the traditional teacher-led or administer-centered learning mainly focuses on getting the learners to perform well on state-mandated tests rather than catering to students' need. This method is a complete failure due to following reasons:

Limiting the teachers' creativity

Teaching from textbooks limits the teachers' creativity in the class. The teachers do not rely firmly on their knowledge and performance. There is a low motivation for innovation in teaching and the effort is to just deliver information or jump directly to the answers. Firstly, teachers cannot choose a coursebook according to their students' needs. Additionally, teachers' teachings are controlled by a fixed curriculum.

Exam or test scores decide the Language Proficiency

The knowledge of students is judged based on their performance in the final exam scores. Since obtaining a higher score is commonly important to both teachers and students, the teaching process is controlled by grading pressure from students, parents, and school principals. Therefore, teachers are pushed to a close system in which all the focus is on getting good marks and performing well on the final exam. Sometimes teachers end up teaching students only the testing purpose as they don't want to lose their prestige due to students' poor performance.

Passive students

In the traditional teacher-centered class all the questions are answered directly by the teacher without students' active involvement. Students should be quiet in the class; in fact, a noisy class means that the teacher cannot manage the class, so she/he is not a good teacher. This is the main reason why teachers avoid noise and student-centered learning, while noise is unavoidable in a student-centered environment due to the exchange of information.

Adding up to, all the reasons for the failure of the Traditional Teaching Methods- Grammar- Translation, Communication -approach, Passive activity, Low energy, Fixed answer mindset, fear of making mistakes, Test scores, limited teachers' creativity, passive students, are also the root cause of English Trauma. In the next chapter, we will understand what is more important- Grammar, Vocabulary, or the Mindset?

CHAPTER THREE

WHAT IS MORE IMPORTANT- GRAMMAR, VOCABULARY, OR MINDSET?

Learners seeking to gain native-like proficiency might be allured to dive headfirst into complex grammar rules. They are wired to think that they won't be able to communicate with foreign colleagues without learning the hard stuff. It's true: it's hard to communicate effectively and smoothly without apt grammar. But without vocabulary, it's impossible.

This is a common debate among the various English trainers as well as learners, what is more, important for fluent English speaking? Vocabulary or grammar. In this chapter, we are going to understand the significance of both along with the mindset which is required while aiming for fluency in English.

VOCABULARY

"While without grammar little can be conveyed, without vocabulary nothing can be conveyed." – David Wilkins

Speaking is one of the most important skills to be developed and enhanced as means of effective communication. Speaking skill is regarded as one of the most difficult aspects of any language learning. Many English learners find it difficult to express themselves in speaking skills. They are generally facing problems to use English to express their thoughts effectively. They struggle in talking because they face psychological obstacles and drawbacks of the traditional learning system (talked about in chapter 2) or cannot find the suitable words and expressions, which means Vocabulary

Language Proficiency depends on Vocabulary size

Studies have shown that, of all the factors contributing to language proficiency, vocabulary size is by far the single most significant factor, accounting for anywhere from 50% to 70% of proficiency gains depending on the language and the skill being studied.

A study analyzes the relationship between receptive vocabulary size in upper-intermediate/advanced learners and EFL (English as a Foreign Language) proficiency and the skills of reading, writing, listening, and speaking. A sample of 42 participants was assessed using a receptive vocabulary size test on ten word-frequency levels (1k to 10k), and on both receptive and productive skills (oral and written). Results reveal that vocabulary size explains language proficiency to a large extent, even in learners with vocabularies of more than 5,000 words, though its influence on performance is not as strong as in learners with smaller vocabularies.

No wonder it is so important, to focus on vocabulary.

You cannot communicate without Vocabulary

As Mr. Wilkins points out above, without basic vocabulary, *you can't say a single word*. Vocabulary is the basic foundation of any language on which grammar, idioms, and other more complex structures can be built.

ESL teacher Keith Folse talks about his adventure at the supermarket in Japan, in his book, *Vocabulary Myths*. He mentions his plan to buy some flour, using the perfect sentence structure, "Sumimasen, ____ -wa Doko desu ka?" (Excuse me, where is the ____?). But he faces one problem: *he doesn't know the word for "flour"*. He discovers one of his Japanese students in the store and asks him for the word. To his bad luck, his student replies "Hana" (flower), not "Kosugi" (flour). He realizes how vital vocabulary can be for simple communication, only after being sent to the floral section. The correct vocabulary word "flour" would have led him to the product. Instead, he ended up with chrysanthemums.

The larger the vocabulary, the easier it is to learn new combinations and sound more like native speakers.

Our brain processes languages using two different memory systems? (Explained in detail later in this Chapter)

Implicit memory:

Implicit memories are those that form without effort.For example, when the lyrics of a popular song get stuck in your head, that's an example of implicit memory at work. You haven't expended any effort to find out the lyrics and melody of the song. Simply hearing it within the background as you set about your day results in the formation of implicit memory.

Explicit memory:

They are things that you intentionally remember and that require conscious effort to bring into memory.This type of memory involves things such as remembering information (Example-grammar rules) for a test, that you have a dentist appointment, and your home address.

Implicit memories are often difficult to explain. If someone asked you how you drive a car or ride a bike, you might struggle to put it into words. You may be able to show them rather explaining them verbally. If they asked you ways to drive to your house, however, you'd probably be ready to articulate the route fairly easily. Remembering the physical process of how to do something (like drive a car) is an implicit memory while remembering the route you have to take to get somewhere is an Explicit memory.

For example, an expression like "She is not really happy with the idea." was traditionally thought to be an exercise in grammar—conjugating "is", negating with "not", applying the preposition "with", the article "the" etc.

But when this is actually processed as a vocabulary "chunk" or a vocabulary phrase, it's easier to remember and practice. The more of those "chunks" you recognize, the less time you would take to process and produce fluent speech. Rather than pertaining to a grammar rule to precise a thought, learners with large vocabularies draw from these pre-constructed chunks, stringing them together into longer, more "native-like" sentences. (I use this technique in my POWER BOOSTER PHRASES course)

It is a fitness exercise that makes you reach the goal of fluency, faster.

Nobody learns a language with the ultimate goal of learning vocabulary. But an outsized vocabulary will cause you to be a far better and fluent speaker, listener, reader, and writer of the language you're learning.

It's a bit like running—many sportsmen sweat on the tracks to train themselves for their sport. It improves their physical fitness. Similarly learning and practicing Vocabulary will make your English-speaking crisp and fit.

Think about how much easier it would be to read a novel in English if you didn't have to look up 10 new words on every page. You won't have to give that blank look or ask people to repeat what they are saying in English, because they used some new and complex words, phrases, slang, or idioms, which you didn't know.

Think about how much flowy your writing would become if you knew some stronger synonyms for words like "good." How fluent your English would sound if you didn't have to repeat words because of low vocabulary. Essentially, you'll be a better communicator if you can understand and be understood!

GRAMMAR

For improving the English language both in and out of the classroom, grammar study is required to an extent. In this section, we are going to understand the value and position of grammar in English language learning and the significance of grammar in the speech and writing process in the English language.

Grammar is not a standalone Subject

Grammar is concerned with how sentences and utterances are formed. In typical English sentences, we will see the 2 most elementary principles of grammar, the arrangements of things (syntax) and therefore the structure of things (morphology). Grammar is neither a separate subject nor is it even a separate division of English work. It's a little part of the English course; that study of the character of the language which helps us to get the "feel" of the language. It is the study of the behavior of words which are reflections of changes in the experiences and sounds of words.

Basic Grammar is required

Learning Tenses, forms of verbs, prepositions, and subject-verb agreement, in other words, basic grammar, is a fundamental requirement for English language students. A student who seeks to get fluency in English; has to study the three tenses of English, its rules, and know-how to apply them in sentences. Also, he has to learn vocabulary words, idioms, and phrases to form sentences.

Some learners believe that the better the grammar, the better is spoken English. That's mistaken. Recall how you acquired your first language. Did you learn lots of grammar rules? You didn't, right? You learned just very basic rules and that too through observation of speech patterns or being corrected by your parents, caretakers, or teachers.

To quote Stephen Krashen, a renowned professor at the University of Southern California and a linguist with lots of work in the field of second-language acquisition:

"Language acquisition doesn't require extensive use of conscious grammatical rules and does not require tedious drills."

Once you recognize basic grammar like tenses, prepositions, different sorts of verbs, and subject-verb agreement, an additional dose of grammar won't shine your spoken English further. What you would like, instead, is more speaking practice. More inputs – listening and reading.

Knowing a language is different from the ability to speak it.

Knowing grammar rules, particularly the above-said tenses, idioms and phrases and vocabulary aids in getting mastery over knowing the English language. Many students equate having the ability to talk in a language with knowing the language and thus view learning the language as learning the way to speak the language. Moreover, 'people have been learning how to learn English instead of speaking English.'

As Nunan (1991) wrote, "success is measured in terms of the ability to carry out a conversation in the (target) language."

Therefore, if students do not learn how to speak (use the grammar they learned) or do not get any opportunity to speak in the language classroom, they may soon get de-motivated and lose interest in learning. A student has to rehearse speech after learning the basic rules of grammar.

One of my students Arav, a technical head in a renowned bank in Abu Dhabi, uses good vocabulary words, phrases & jargon. He has detailed knowledge about his profession. Also, he is confident enough to speak in front of people in English. But the only reason why he is unable to impress people with his language skills is his inability to weave his thoughts and words together properly. For which certainly you need basic grammar understanding.

Based on a sample of more than 30,000 students from 500+ colleges in India, National Spoken English Skills Report by Aspiring Minds paints quite a poor picture:

"...a dismal 25% of candidates understand the usage of basic grammar constructs, like the right use of articles and tenses."

According to the report, lack of grammar skills is the third biggest problem in spoken English after fluency and pronunciation. Only 18.7% of candidates have reasonably good grammar skills.

Grammar plays a far more important role in writing than in speaking. Grammar rules do help in certain limited situations: good 'grammar' users can apply conscious rules when they have time to think about and use them, as in writing, but even here research indicates that grammar use makes a very modest contribution to grammatical accuracy. For most people, using 'grammar' in real conversation only leads to trouble. Constantly referring to rules gives one a very hesitant style of speaking that is not pleasant to listen to, and some of us have the bad habit of constructing our sentences via grammar rules while the other person is talking, which means that we are not listening! The best way to imbibe these rules is to regularly read and listen to English.

The focus should be on Grammar acquisition

Alternatively, if the right activities for Grammar acquisition rather than learning, are taught in the right way, speaking English can be a lot easier, less traumatic, less stressful, automatic, subconscious, and more fun, raising general learner motivation and making the

English language classroom a fun and dynamic place to be.

MIND-SET- Stop analyzing

You must have learned English using those traditional learning systems. Did you memorize vocabulary word lists? Did you fill in the blanks with word forms? Did you learn advanced grammar, pronunciation rules, and tenses that you'll never use except on a test? It is a challenge to remember the grammar rules, and vocabulary lists so learned in school, in college, or even in a private class, especially if you haven't practiced them much since you finished studying. If we don't practice, we lose those language skills. We have discussed in Chapter 2, the reasons for the failure of the traditional methods of learning. So that's completely not your fault!

The traditional way of learning might prepare you for tests, for quizzes in a textbook, or maybe for the TOEFL or IELTS. They might prepare you for a diploma in high school or a college degree, but they don't prepare you for the real world.

My Belief

One of the main principles of the TURBO ENGLISH MASTERY program is not to analyze your speech from a grammatical perspective. The same applies to reading. You may try to understand what a specific sentence, states as per English grammar concepts, and the absurd side to it are, that sometimes you are simply confused instead of achieving something! You read a sentence and your left brain starts analyzing automatically: "Wait wait, is it a passive or active voice structure? Is it a dependent clause or an independent clause?" Then you go to refer to a grammar textbook or Google and try to find out! You end up browsing various websites & killing your time to meet your curiosity! Wasting a lot of time and learning absolutely nothing.

The good news is you are not alone. There are millions of English learners who think of such questions. The moment they come across a new sentence, they try to understand, "how some words and groups are being used in that sentence? Which Grammar tense is being used in the given sentence? So on and so forth.

I remember the times when I analyzed everything, that I read or heard, and I don't feel shy to mention that this was the core reason I couldn't speak English fluently. My mind was following a permanent analytical regime, and I lived under a false impression that, when I become a master in English grammar, I would be able to speak English fluently. So, I did all I could to improve my grammar, read books, solved grammar exercises, and watched YouTube videos related to all the grammar perspectives. Then one day I got a chance to talk with someone in English, and you know what? I still spoke very poorly. I wanted to say something, it was in my head but I couldn't get the words and when I finally managed to speak, I felt that I was making a lot of grammatical errors. Despite studying so much grammar my spoken English was still poor. WHY? Because I was caught up in the **Analysis-Paralysis.**

I didn't realize that it was completely wrong logic. Just think about it – Will the ability to define, what a certain set of words represent, help you to create that phrase or sentence when writing or speaking in English? For sure, It will not.

BUT why is it? Let's find out by answering a simple question. Do you think your knowledge of English is- automatic, without conscious effort, subconscious or it is thinking, focussing, paying attention, and being conscious?

Knowledge of English- Implicit or Explicit?

When you learn something, new knowledge is created in your brain. There are two types of knowledge, Implicit knowledge and Explicit knowledge. If you want to speak fluently in English you must know the difference between the two.

Implicit knowledge

Implicit knowledgeis automatic, without conscious attention. Examples of such activities are: Riding a bicycle, playing a musical instrument, and speaking your native language. It is fast automatic and effortless, that is why you ride a bicycle without focusing on the movement of your legs. That is the reason why singers can sing while still playing musical instruments without paying attention to their fingers and that is the reason why you can speak your native language easily effortlessly and automatically naturally without focusing on any grammar rules. That's possible because of implicit knowledge.

Explicit knowledge

Explicit knowledge is the opposite of implicit knowledge. It is a knowledge that requires conscious thinking focusing attention and you need to think you need to focus on it before doing anything which involves explicit knowledge for example: Solving a math problem. Suppose I give you 34 x 18 you cannot answer it automatically without calculating, on a calculator or your brain, you need time to think. Unless you are an Abacus student. Another example can be, telling the names of states of India- it requires effort. Or explaining a grammar rule, which will obviously take time to think and explain.

It's only useful when you are doing a task that doesn't require a quick response. This type of knowledge is futile when it comes to spoken English where you have to answer instantaneously, you have to react quickly to a question or a remark.

For example, someone asks you "Where have you been last night?" now before answering you start thinking, OK, the question is about last night I am supposed to answer in the past tense and I want to say "I was in a mall". Now should I say A Mall or The Mall? Because my grammar teacher told me to say "The Mall". Obviously, you don't have time to revise think and apply all these grammar rules. That makes sense, right?

So, if you want to speak good English you must stop doing activities that result in explicit knowledge for example:

1. Watching a video explaining the difference between can and could.

2. Reading an article that teaches you the usage of a, an & the.

3. Listening to a lecture that teaches you the usage of prepositions at, on, in, & of.

Following these activities can definitely improve your writing skills but obviously not your speaking. Implicit knowledge is automatic so you don't have to think about grammar while speaking this allows you to concentrate on expressing your thoughts and ideas. As a result, you can speak English effortlessly. It feels as if you are talking in your native language

Most of the English learners cannot distinguish, (and it's all due to the kind of teaching traditional English at school!) between the Explicit or Theoretical knowledge (which is using Grammar rules, syntax, tenses, prepositions, and articles) and the Implicit knowledge (the skills and ability to use English automatically, when speaking or writing! Without conscious efforts and analysis)

Repeat, don't Learn

Many of us believe that knowledge transforms directly into skills - but that's not how it happens! The ability to speak, for example, depends upon your ability to repeat correct speech patterns, and the best way to meet it is only by imitating and remembering a particular sentence. If you talk to real people in real life, is someone really interested in whether the sentences are active or passive?

NO!

All that is important is your ability to say it out LOUD! You will never find me posting any articles related to Grammar and its usage. Use of present continuous tenses, the difference between could have or should have, where to use A, An, The.

According to me, grammar knowledge actually doesn't matter that much – it's all about your ability to replicate grammatically correct English patterns. Well, I don't want to mislead my readers by talking about grammar first and then telling them that they actually don't need the grammar. The truth is the basic grammar you've learned is enough to help you become a good English speaker. So, STOP studying grammar anymore.

To be honest, I have actually forgotten most of the Grammar terms, rules, and definitions. Understand that, "Just Having an explicit knowledge of Grammar rules and theories will not serve the PRACTICAL PURPOSE".

Real-life English

When you speak in real life with real people, you don't have time for APPLYING the grammar rules! Yes, you might be building sentences in your brain, from the scratch - especially if you're a struggling English speaker - but you still have to agree that knowing the role of a particular word or group of words in a sentence - "predicate", "adjective" or "conditionals" - WILL NOT help you build that sentence.

The average native English speakers have no idea about all of the grammar, still, they are fluent! They USE English words and phrases without even exactly knowing their role in a sentence and that's the major reason, why I stopped caring about grammar rules, years ago. And imagine, this does not prevent me from helping other English learners!

Fluency is your ability to speak without thinking, without hesitation, and at a comfortable pace. So, the next time you catch yourself asking a question like - "What's the predicate and what's the subject in this sentence? ..." - give it a thought.

CHAPTER FOUR

ENGLISH SPEAKING-SCIENCE OR ARTS?

"I'm enough of an artist to draw freely on my imagination. Imagination is more important than knowledge. Knowledge is limited; imagination encircles the world."- Einstein

In this chapter, we will try to understand the relationship between the science and the arts of English speaking. Formal knowledge of a language is an important part of learning, but ultimately the utterances are dependent upon your boundless imagination and creativity.

Is English Speaking a science?

Science is a theoretical subject that studies how everything functions and how something comes into being. For example, give a person oxygen and hydrogen molecules. Also, provide all facilities to make these molecules interact according to a set procedure to make water. You will observe that he must follow an equivalent procedure; otherwise, he cannot hope to form water from hydrogen and oxygen molecules. You will see that every person who attempts to make water must follow the same procedure; otherwise, he cannot hope to make water from hydrogen and oxygen molecules. What we can understand from this experiment is this. If we have the same input and same procedure to achieve an output, the output will always be the same, uniform, and standardized

Quite similar to this, the traditional teaching methods make us believe that there is a standard way or procedure to produce sentences in English. So, is English speaking a science?

Science makes you think about everything in a practical form. We end up justifying everything. It forces us to think that the beautiful green leaf that is there on a tree is not added to it just to add beauty to the environment. It is there to provide food to the tree through photosynthesis. A scientist tries to justify his or her creations.

Similarly, the traditional learning method, makes us more concerned about the creation of sentences accurately. We end up justifying our speech as right or wrong instead of paying attention to the beauty of our thoughts and ideas. So, is English speaking a science?

A standardized English may limit the speakers' abilities.

English speaking is not a subject like science or maths which you can learn, you can apply formulas and the answer you get will either be wrong or right. English speaking is a skill which you need to learn and do. Every time you do it, every time you perform it you become better and more proficient at it.

In his book "The Natural Approach", Dr. Stephen Krashen mentions, "It is almost a paradox that what man seems perfectly equipped to do when the need and opportunity arise- acquire the ability to communicate in another language – seems elusive to language classes and instructors"

One of my students Divya worked in a call center of a production house. Every day, she had to receive calls for taking orders and providing the clients with the dispatch details. She was trained with a standardized procedure and a fixed communication technique to deal with every client. She shares the humiliating story of the day when her conversation went wrong because the client asked some questions that she was not prepared to answer. The fixed answer method had limited her creativity and understanding. She was unable to frame sentences differently according to the conversation.

Additionally, research by the Social Sciences and Humanities Research Council of Canada, shows that these procedures are not universal. Language, or more broadly communication, is understood as a key component of work-related competence, whether objectified as a skill or rendered invisible as a talent.

In her work on an Ontario call center, Roy (2003) showed how several language-related competencies were treated in ways similar to other forms of work-related competence. For example, all procedures, including interaction with clients, were standardized (cf. also Cameron 2001); French-English bilingualism was treated as a knowledge set in exactly the same way as, say, knowledge regarding the company's automobile service sector; linguistic proficiency was subject to standardized testing.

Service providers were meant to reach clients, but since clients rarely come in one size, it was difficult to find standardized routines that correspond to a wide variety of ways of speaking (or writing).

Studying English as a Science or a Subject makes it seem difficult.

The English language is often full of disparities and illogical statements. Many words confuse non-native speakers. To exemplify, what relation does pineapple have with the words "pine" and "apple"?

There are also cases where nouns become verbs. Teachers, for example, taught while trainers trained. It's quite difficult for a native English speaker to clarify. So, imagine how difficult it is for English learners to understand these variances.

Complex Rules and Exceptions:

The English language, like any other, is abundant with rules. Whether they're the grammar rules, exceptions to the rules, or the spelling rules. There are many of them. And there are many ways for them to get changed, disproved, or proved wrong. For example, one of the spelling rules of English we learned explains "I" before "E" except after "C." When it comes to most English words, such as "friend" and "believe," this rule stands true. There are, however, exceptions, such as "science" and "wierdness."

Words Order:

When we consider sentence order, there are several confusing rules to know. Native speakers have an intuitive knowledge of the way to order those words because they sound correct.

It's not clear why the words are set in such a way that they sound right. You may say "an interesting small cup," but "a small interesting cup" does not sound right. English has very subtle word ordering rules that make "A cute little brown dog" correct to say, whereas "A brown cute little dog" would be incorrect.

You can immediately detect the order of the words if you speak English fluently. Another difficulty for learners is distinguishing between right and incorrect orders. While it's grammatically correct, the way it sounds distinguishes how it's going to be delivered. Native speakers, for example, have an intuitive grasp of the language's complexities.

Verb Forms

Irregular verbs in English seem to be complex and are often stressful for English learners. Why is the past tense of "buy" "bought", and why is the past tense of "sell" "sold." Why aren't "buyed" nor "selled" real words?

Writing Rules:

Even native English speakers make mistakes, especially when it involves punctuation rules. It's the stylistic side of writing that provides them the most trouble. Whether it's the fast Oxford

Comma of today or how to use hyphens in compound nouns. There's always something new to learn. This field of English requires the most focus of all the language skills.

The strange case of the English pronoun "I" is additionally worth mentioning. When we consider all other English pronouns, we will observe that "I" is the only one written in capital letters, regardless of its form.

Confusing Spellings:

English is fundamentally difficult to learn in certain ways. One explanation is that English has a crazy perplexing spelling system and it seems like every word makes up its own pronunciation rules because English has borrowed so many words from other languages. Even native speakers find it confusing. In order to understand the way to read the spelling you've got to; understand which language it comes from or you may have previously heard the accurate pronunciation.

For instance, the words' dough,' 'tough,' and 'bough' all have precise spelling but are pronounced differently. This '-ough' spelling is a relic from Middle English, Chaucer's country. Where the spelling reflected the pronunciation.

Many of those pronunciations have changed over time. But the spelling remained constant. Like the 'ch' sound within the Scottish word 'loch,' it's not used in British English pronunciation anymore.

Confusing Idioms:

Idioms are another tricky topic to learn. Every language contains idioms. They aren't meant to take literally. For example, the phrase "she kicked the bucket" means "she died." All you need to know is the meaning of the whole unit.

'Getting on my nerves,' or 'cut the Corner,' are two other examples. The literal sense is not the exact wording. Also, Idioms include words like 'in the blink of an eye,' which a language learner does not understand.

In English, there is a multitude of these. Idioms exist in all languages. The length, variety, and unpredictability of English idioms are their typical characteristic. Idioms in English are tricky for non-native speakers to grasp.

It's Difficult to Use Plurals and Tenses:

Since there are numerous tenses to notice. Often it is difficult for an English learner to differentiate between future tense and future perfect tense.

It is difficult to learn while memorizing grammar rules in the text. Also, while having an English conversation during which the speaker refers to the future.

Furthermore, when it involves the usage of plurals in English, there are several variations. When it involves words like child and tooth, where a non-native speaker learns to add -s to form a plural, this is the wrong English.

Synonyms Aren't Always Synonymous:

If you check out a thesaurus, you'll find several groups of words that generally have a similar meaning. If you think this meant they could be used interchangeably, then you are mistaken. Since English words may have various meanings. Even terms with very similar definitions can refer to something entirely different.

People may misuse a word as a result of this. You will "see a film" or "watch television," but you would never "see a television." Another example is, you may say, "I received a present," you don't say, "I welcomed a present."

Albeit the two words are similar in referring to the background, the context could be entirely different.

Different Dialects:

We assume that every language has a regional dialect. Due to the various regional dialects in the U.K, people find it challenging to learn English. There is a distinct north/south distinction when pronouncing "bath" or "castle.". In the south, it's an extended "A," while in the north, it's a short "A." And there is an ever-lasting debate on the way to pronounce 'scone' correctly (S-gone or S-cone?).

Of course, each English-speaking nation has its unique way of pronouncing words. The U.S., India, Canada, Australia, and South Africa each have their specific way of pronouncing words. This means that the place where you study English has a huge impact on the pronunciation you use.

It can be utterly challenging for people, who are trying to learn the language, to get used to all the complex rules and exceptions to the rules. Rules don't always work. Especially when trying to use traditional knowledge to apply the same rule to a new word. Major problems arise when the beginners become overconcerned with the correctness of real-life communications, trying to cross-check their speech patterns against conscious rules at all times. This concern leads to hesitation, broken sentences unnatural, and synthetic English.

English speaking is an Art

Art is a very free area where you get to observe the environment, creatures as well as your thoughts. You can choose to create and show people in whatever way you wish to. Here are some examples to help you understand what art is all about.

Give a piece of paper, all colors, and a brush, and ask different people to come up with a picture of the rocky mountain from a distance. The number of answers you will get to the question asked, will be equivalent to the people willing to answer. This is because every person has his individual perception of the Rocky Mountains, and thus, uses various color mixes to come up with a picture that he feels best relates to the original.

Give steel, tires, engine, and other internal parts and ask different people to make a car. You will be surprised to see as many different-looking cars as there are people accepting the challenge.

What these experiments clearly demonstrate is the fact that we can create a thing using the same input and different processes. The output is not standard and depends upon people's perceptions. This is what we refer to as art.

"Art is a way of communicating an idea, whether it is done through music, painting, sculpture, or dance. The goal of "art" is to communicate an idea." The goal of "language" is to be able to use a language proficiently to communicate an idea. English as a language, is just a tool, a medium of conveying your thoughts and imaginations. How can we expect to fence these ideas, thoughts, experiences, and suggestions within the boundaries of rules and fixed answers? We need to give them the wings of creativity and imagination. Any language is an ocean of structures, lexical resources, words, and phrases. There are more than 100 ways of saying the same thing. So how can there be a fixed answer? All you need to do is be creative and fill the canvas of your communication with the colors of imagination.

The persistent question in the context of creativity has always been whether the defining factors come from nature or nurture. So definitely, all human beings are born with some level of creativity which they acquire from nature, DNA, or genes, all you need is to nurture it.

Similarly, every human being is born with an understanding of semantics and syntax which is known as Universal Grammar (Explained in Chapter 5). All you need is to nurture it with proper practice. So, learning the basic foundational rules of a language is essential but then you have to blend it with your creativity.

"After a certain high level of technical skill is achieved, science and art tend to coalesce in aesthetics, plasticity, and form. The greatest scientists are always artists as well." --Remark made in 1923; recalled by Archibald Henderson, Durham Morning Herald, August 21, 1955; Einstein Archive 33-257.

English speaking is easy.

Often, I come across students saying, "English is such a difficult language." According to me, this is all in your head. If you have an opinion that English is a difficult language then you will search and find every reason to justify your belief that it is hard to learn. But if you believe that it is easy to learn then you will find reasons to justify that belief.

English speaking is an art, it's a skill that you can acquire through exposure to the language and meaningful communication, without the need for systematic studies of any kind.

"The mistake the beginners make is to assume that a conscious understanding of grammar is a prerequisite to acquiring communicative competence in English."

One of my students Mr. Shobhit Das, who is a head in the department of international affairs in a reputed Company, shares, "I completed my schooling from a Bengali medium school, where English Grammar was taught in a scholarly way. Every concept of grammar was crystal clear to me. I scored pretty good marks in the subject. It was only when I moved into the college and tried to speak in English, that I found my Grammar knowledge was useless"

What is most important is your need or desire to acquire the language and the ability to use it for real communicative purposes. All you need to do is STOP learning and start acquiring English. Just as you have acquired your native language.

Language Acquisition

Acquiring a language means "picking it up", which means developing ability in English by using it in natural real-life conversations. You have acquired your first language or your native language. Children acquire their mother tongue through interaction with their parents and the environment that surrounds them. Their urge to communicate paves the way for language acquisition to occur.

As experts suggest, every human being has an innate capacity to acquire language. Language acquisition Is the natural way to develop linguistic ability and is a SUBCONSCIOUS PROCESS. For example, while acquiring your native language, you are not aware of the process, you are just communicating and focussing on your ideas.

English studying is absolutely different from the acquisition. It means knowing the rules, having conscious knowledge of grammar, and possessing formal knowledge of various aspects of English. English study gives you an "explicit knowledge ". It is a conscious process; you know the rules moreover you can talk about them consciously.

Whereas Acquisition of English is "implicit learning". As we discussed earlier implicit Knowledge is fast, automatic, subconscious, and effortless. It is so because after learning you have practiced it so well. The skill you have learned is not a burden, fear, or stress for you. You enjoy the process of learning and application.

For this, you need to invest yourself in the process of acquiring English. In the upcoming chapters, you will understand how you can keep daily contact with English and incorporate it into your lifestyle. You can accomplish anything, no matter how difficult it may seem, if you consistently apply yourself to it and are committed to the result. "NASA didn't bother to ask whether it was difficult to place a human on the moon, they asked whether it is possible and discovered ways to make it happen."

English learning is not a destination with a unique and smooth path to follow, it is a journey that will lead you down many different paths. English will seem easy for you when you stop looking at it as something mechanical and start connecting with the language on a deeper level by trying to acquire it.

CHAPTER FIVE

Human Brain & Language Acquisition

Can a mouse except Stuart Little talk about his feelings and express his enthusiasm in words?

Human beings are the only species on this planet who can communicate using Language. Whereas other species do possess an innate ability to communicate by producing a limited number of meaningful vocalizations (e.g. bonobos), or even through partially learned systems (e.g. bird songs), there is no other species that may exist that can express ideas (sentences) with a limited set of symbols (speech sounds and words).

Just imagine, holding and admiring a baby in your hand. Trying to pacify him with all the gibberish utterances. You know that it won't understand a word you say, much less talk to you. What kind of magic happens, that transforms this absolutely ignorant chap into a goblin who can tease his schoolmate to tears? A passionate lover who can woo his girl with poems. A motivational blogger whose 2000 words write-up can put a fire under the readers.

It is through Language acquisition. It is the process of building the ability to understand a language, and using it to communicate with others. Language acquisition, more specifically, relates to first language or native language acquisition. If you were born in China and your parents, neighbors, caretakers, and everyone speaks in Mandarin with you, you'll naturally end up talking Mandarin. The same applies to whatever native language you're taught.

After you've acquired your native tongue, another language acquisition happens after that—which is called "second language acquisition." The reason why you've picked up this book is, that you want to acquire English as your second language.

Were you given a long list of vocabulary words to memorize or a thick grammar textbook to study and solve exercises, when you learned your native tongue? You were just with people all around speaking in your native tongue in all the daily life casual conversations. You were totally immersed in the language and you learned it probably unconsciously. Moreover, you can't even remember how you picked up your native tongue.

When it comes to English, the methods used in traditional training are quite different from what happens in the native language. You consciously study grammar. You prepare your word lists with their flashcards and translations. You refer to apps, websites, podcasts, and YouTube videos that teach you grammar and vocabulary.

The good news is, that you can acquire English as your second language just as you acquired your native language. It's not that second language acquisition is unnatural or that it's only for the gifted. It's just that we need better tools and methods to do it, and we'll talk about all of them in this book.

But, how does the process of Language Acquisition, actually take place in the mind of a language learner? Whether it's first or second language acquisition. Psychologists and linguists have propounded a multitude of theories over the decades to explain the phenomenon, and we're going to look into three of the most influential ones in this Chapter.

1. Behaviorism (B.F. Skinner)

B.F. Skinner (1957), one of the pioneers of behaviorism, provides one of the earliest scientific explanations, that language acquisition is really one big and complex case of behavior therapy. He accounted for language development through environmental influence. Skinner argued that children learn language supported by behaviorist reinforcement principles by associating words with meanings. Correct utterances are positively reinforced when the kid realizes the communicative value of words and phrases. At its core, it's all pattern recognition—associating words with meaning.

For instance, if a baby hears the word "milk" often enough right before being fed from the bottle, he'll soon learn what that word means. When the child says 'milk' and the mother will smile and give her some as a result, the child will find this outcome rewarding, enhancing the child's language development.

If he always hears the word "ball" right before being handed a spherical object, he'll begin to associate "ball" with its referent.

A child (or a second language learner) will eventually be able to learn correct grammar, through a process of trial and error. According to this, Language acquisition is a stimulus-response mechanism. A child will pick up the correct form of the language when he observes a reinforcing positive behavior from those around him—a smile, a nod, or being handed a spherical object when he says "ball." These actions satisfy him that he's correct in his assumptions.

Another quick way of going to the correct form or use of the language, rather than going at it through personal trial and error, is imitation. A baby can simply imitate what an adult says or how she says it. That's why accents can be contagious. Most of the students from West Bengal have a typical Bengali accent. They show Extreme MTI (Mother Tongue Influence) in their English pronunciations.

Finally, in the behaviorist's view, language is simply a reinforced input. Either through Trial and Error or imitation.

2. Universal Grammar (Dr. Naom Chomsky)

However, in the 1960s, Skinner's account of behaviorism was soon heavily attacked by Noam Chomsky, the world's most famous linguist to date. A man recognized as the father of modern linguists.

He indicated that if you really look closer, an adult native speaker of a language knows things he could not have learned from the samples of speech he has heard. According to Chomsky, parents give only very little linguistic input for kids to learn a language. Interactions between a parent and a child are limited to repeated utterances of things like "Take this", "Bring it here" and "Open your mouth". They are not very likely to make a significant impact on language learning.

For example, when a child says, "I swimmed today," he didn't really get that from any adult person around him in his life. That's not imitation. Consider these two sentences, 'Is the program that's on television any good? ' and 'Is the program that on television is good? ' A speaker of English immediately knows that the former sentence can possibly be used and that the latter cannot be used; he knows in some sense that the 'is ' that's shifted to the start of a sentence during a question comes out of the main clause, instead of the subordinate clause. So how could he have acquired this piece of information about English?

A few sentences that a child may have come across are, 'The program is good ', "The program that is on television is good ', 'Is the program good? ', and so on. None of those show the rule being broken; they provide him information about what he *can* say, not about what he *can't* say. The rule can be demonstrated to exist only by concocting an ungrammatical sentence that would never occur in real life, 'Is the program that on television is good? ', or by giving a grammatical analysis. But these are the sorts of information that the child learning his native language precisely *doesn't* have available to him.

Chomsky argues, that if native speakers find the sentence ungrammatical, their judgement must be based on something other than the external input, something that is not from outside. Then the remaining possibility is that it is derived from some property of the human mind that they all share.

Consequently, he proposed the theory of Universal Grammar: an idea of innate, biological grammatical categories, such as a noun category and a verb category that facilitate the entire language development in children and overall language processing in adults. The language properties inherent in the human mind make up 'Universal Grammar ', which consists, not of particular rules or a particular grammar, but of a set of general principles that apply to all grammar and that leave certain parameters open; Universal Grammar sets the limits within which human languages can vary.

One way of visualizing Universal Grammar is to ascertain it as part of the brain. Language acquisition is the growth of the mental organ of language triggered by certain language experiences. Hence the idea of Universal Grammar is usually mentioned as part of biology.

How to nurture and nourish it with various language experiences, which we will discuss in the coming chapters.

Language Acquisition Device (LAD)

He also propounded the "Innate Hypothesis Theory". According to this, Linguistic ability is innate to us. Chomsky asserts that humans are biologically wired for language—that they have a "language acquisition device" that enables them to learn any language in the world.

Chomsky would argue that children use this "language acquisition device" to figure out the rules specific to their native language with the help of Universal Grammar.

LAD is a hypothetical tool that is present in the brain by birth. It helps the children rapidly understand and learn any language. This is responsible for amazingly quick acquisition of language abilities and understanding of grammar, semantics, and syntax.

Let us understand it this way, the brain has got templates for all languages. Once it gets in contact with a particular language environment, it catches that particular language, and that language becomes our mother tongue. The other templates that remain unused for an extended period of time, are eventually lost.

So, the language learning capability is already there in the child when he/she is born. Normally the children internalize their mother tongue even before going to school, before learning any grammar rules. How do they do so? Because they are surrounded by people- parents, caretakers, and teachers, who speak in their native language. The only thing they require is a conducive environment or proper exposure to that language in order to master it.

3. Second language Acquisition Theory (Dr. Stephen Krashen)

The second language acquisition theory is the brainchild of renowned linguist and researcher, Stephen Krashen. The theory was put forth in the 1980s, where it was influencing all research into how a second language is acquired. He explained the methodology of the "Natural Approach" which is followed largely in all areas of second language research and teaching forms the base for the Turbo English Mastery Program.

"Language acquisition does not require extensive use of conscious grammatical rules, and does not require tedious drill."- Stephen Krashen

According to the theory, one does not need to use grammatical rules of the target language extensively in order to learn it. All that is required are meaningful interactions in the language, which generally focuses more on the message that is conveyed than the grammar and rules of speech. Competence in the language is acquired as a result of receiving comprehensible input without having undergone any formal instruction or training on the grammar or reading of the language.

Krashen's theory of second language acquisition consists of five main hypotheses:

- the **Acquisition-Learning** hypothesis;
- the **Monitor** hypothesis;
- the **Input** hypothesis;
- and the **Affective Filter** hypothesis;
- the **Natural Order** hypothesis.

*1. The **Acquisition-Learning** hypothesis*

According to this hypothesis, an adult can develop a second language competence in two ways. Firstly, via "Language Acquisition". This is the product of a **subconscious process** or implicit knowledge, very similar to the way the children acquire their first language. It requires meaningful interaction in the target language - natural or real-life communication - in which speakers are concentrated not in the form of their utterances, but in the communicative act. In this, the student develops the "Feeling of correctness"

Secondly, through "Language learning", which is the product of formal instruction and it comprises of a **conscious process** that results in conscious formal knowledge 'about' the language, for example, knowledge of grammar rules. Being aware of the rules and being able to talk about them.

A deductive approach in a teacher-centered setting produces "**learning**", while an inductive approach in a student-centered setting leads to "**acquisition**".

According to Dr. Krashen 'learning' is less important than 'acquisition'.

*2. The **Monitor** hypothesis*

As per this theory, formal knowledge or conscious learning has a limited function in adult second language performance. It is used only as a monitor or an editor. It proves that whatever we speak in a second language is due to an acquired system. The fluency in speaking thus comes from what we have picked up subconsciously, in natural communicative situations. The role of formal knowledge is just to check or repair correction on the output which is the result of the acquired system.

The function of 'monitor' is to act in planning, editing, and correcting functions while speaking English when three specific conditions are met:

- Second language learner has sufficient time at their disposal.
- They focus on form or think about correctness.
- They know the rule.

It appears that the role of conscious learning is quite limited in second language performance. According to Krashen, the role of the monitor is minimal, being used only to correct deviations from "normal" speech and to give the speech a more 'polished' appearance.

Krashen also suggests that 'monitor' use may vary from one language learner to another. He distinguishes those learners into 3 categories

- Over-users: Those who use the 'monitor' all the time. They are introverts and perfectionists. Lack of self-confidence is frequently related to the over-use of the "monitor".
- under-users: Those learners who have not learned or who prefer not to use their conscious knowledge. They are usually extroverts.
- optimal users: Those learners that use the 'monitor' appropriately.

An evaluation of the person's psychological profile can help to determine to what group they belong

*3. The **Input** hypothesis*

The **Input** hypothesis is Krashen's attempt to explain how we acquire a second language – how second language acquisition takes place. The Input hypothesis is only concerned with 'acquisition', not 'learning'. The hypothesis claims that ability to speak or write fluently in a second language will come on its own with time. Fluency emerges gradually and cannot be taught directly.

The input hypothesis claims the importance of listening comprehension and reading comprehension in a language learning program. According to this hypothesis, the learner improves and progresses along with the 'natural order' when he/she receives second language 'input' that is one step beyond his/her current stage of linguistic competence. For example, if a learner is at a stage 'i', then acquisition takes place when he/she is exposed to **'Comprehensible Input'** that belongs to level 'i + 1'. Since not all the learners can be at the same level of linguistic competence at the same time, Krashen suggests that *natural communicative input* is the key to designing a syllabus, ensuring in this way that each learner will receive some 'i + 1' input that is appropriate for his/her current stage of linguistic competence.

Acquisition occurs best when the learner is exposed to the second level input at a slightly higher level than they are competent at. This is done with the help of context. Comprehensible input refers to the information which is understood by the learner. Input in which focus is on the message not on the grammatical forms.

*4. The **Affective Filter** hypothesis*

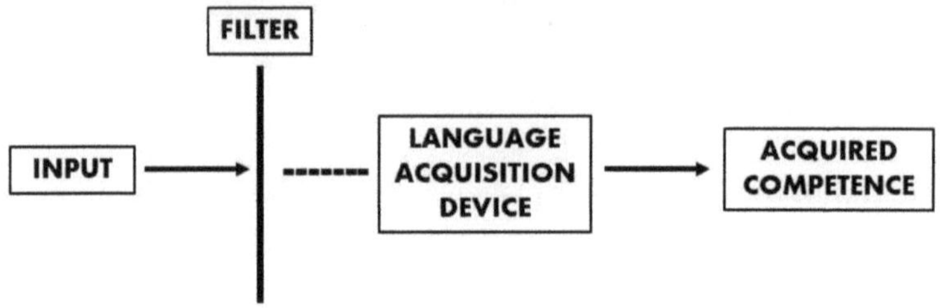

The Affective filter. "the Natural Approach"- Dr. Stephen Krashen

The **Affective Filter** hypothesis represents Krashen's view that several 'affective variables' plays a facilitative, but non-causal, role in second language acquisition. These variables include motivation, self-confidence, anxiety, and personality traits. Krashen claims that learners with high motivation, self-confidence, a good self-image, a low level of anxiety, and extroversion are better equipped for success in second language acquisition. Whereas, low motivation, low self-esteem, anxiety, introversion, and inhibition can raise the affective filter and form a 'mental block' that prevents comprehensible input from reaching the LAD. In other words, when the filter is 'up' it obstructs language acquisition. On the other hand, positive affect is necessary, for the acquisition to take place.

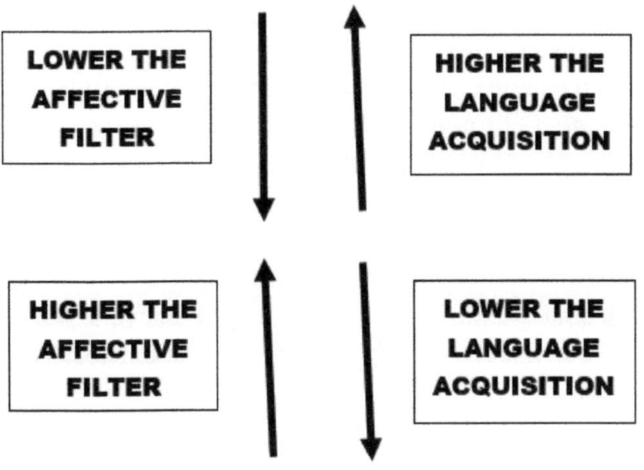

5. The Natural Order hypothesis.

Finally, the **Natural Order** hypothesis suggested that the acquisition (not learning) of grammatical structures follows a 'natural order' which is predictable. It does not state that every acquirer will acquire grammatical structures in the exact same order. Certain structures tend to be acquired early while some are acquired late. This order seemed to be independent of the learners' age, L1 background, and conditions of exposure, and although the agreement between individual acquirers was not always 100% in the studies, there were statistically significant similarities that reinforced the existence of a Natural Order of language acquisition. Krashen rejects grammatical sequencing when the goal is language acquisition. By allowing student errors to occur without emphasizing error correction the natural order is allowed to take its course.

These theories are related to each other in various ways. All of them are the crux of extensive research and study. These are universally acceptable and form the basis of Second Language Acquisition. The theories prove that your brain has an inbuilt capacity for language acquisition. All you need is to keep supplying comprehensible input to it. The other very important thing is your attitude and mindset towards the language.

So, if you are seeking to learn English as your second Language, Better consider acquiring it naturally instead of learning it externally like a subject. This chapter was an explanation of the relationship between the human brain and language acquisition. In the next chapter, we are going to discuss how should you learn English to be able to speak it naturally, automatically, and subconsciously.

CHAPTER SIX

How to Acquire English? - Like Babies Do!

As an adult, you have an incredible cognitive advantage. You're better at problem-solving you have more general knowledge. You have more cognitive power. You're just smarter than a baby in every single way. So why can't you use this power to learn a language? Well, the reason is quite surprising. The reason is that you know too much. Especially if you know too much about language. So, every time you try to speak you are putting all that knowledge into use.

Let's imagine language from the perspective of a baby. For example, a mother asks a baby to say "mama, mama". The baby may just be making lip movements. Mom again asks him to say "mama", "mama mama". He may end up saying "mama" or something else. So, babies don't know anything about the language. They don't know the difference between nouns and verbs and adjectives and prepositions. They don't understand future tense and past tense. all they hear is sound, continuous sound. A big long noise.

Just think about it. Maybe it's a question you've never really thought about, how do babies and children know what you're talking about? How do they know how to take a noun, a word for a thing? How do they know how to take that out of a sentence? How do they learn verbs when it's all just joined together?

The answer is that they don't know.

This is the natural way of learning English. The best learners in the world are -babies and small children. They comfortably learn to speak like a native speaker with excellent grammar, vocabulary, fluency, and pronunciation rather than studying textbooks. In other words, they learn the language subconsciously and naturally. Perhaps we should look at babies and understand how they learn English.

What can we learn from babies?

1. The "Silent Period"

When a baby first starts to learn English or any language, it mostly just listens. In fact, for many months the baby or the child will only listen without any real speaking. This period of listening is called the "silent Period" by the linguists. During this period the baby is just learning to understand the language. So the babies get an understanding of the different tones, rhythms, and sounds of a language during this silent period.

Listening is most important for language acquisition. It's the first language skill humans develop. Without listening, they'd have no building blocks from which they can build their own repetition of sounds. And yet, how many traditional language teaching programs focus on the significance of listening as a central skill, as opposed to grammar or vocabulary?

The reason may be that listening seems to be unreliable. It seems like nothing's happening. It's too passive an activity, unlike speaking. When speaking you actually can hear what was learned. The benefits of listening are initially not heard.

In contrast to common belief, listening should be an intensely active activity. So as an English learner, you need to devote time to actively listening to English. Listening is quite powerful, similar to the silent period it helps you in language acquisition, which is a subconscious process.

The diagram below, as published in The Criterion an International Journal in English represents the significance of active listening. The process of listening occurs in five stages. They are hearing, understanding, remembering, evaluating, and responding.

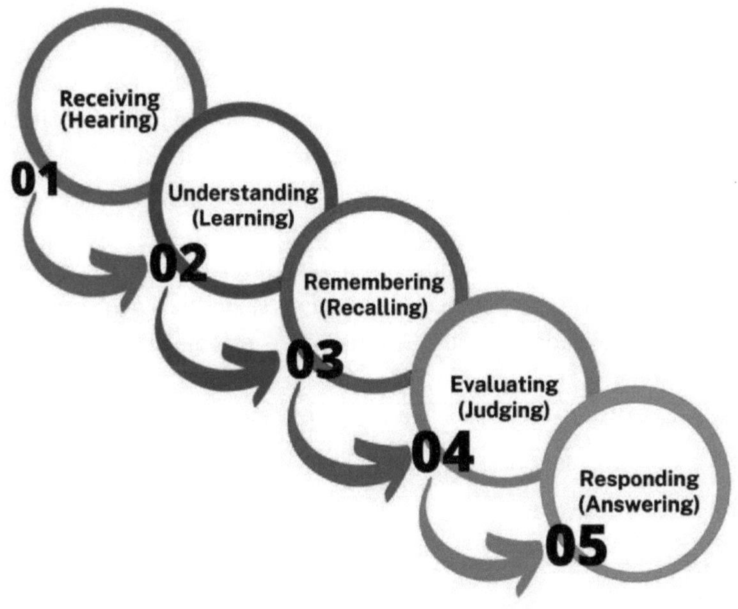

5 stages in the listening process.

2. The power of Imagination

Young children have incredible imaginations. We experience that in the stories they tell and the "trouble" they get into as they explore and make sense of their words. People become less imaginative and less creative as they get older. It's just part of growing up...or so we are told.

Unfortunately, our capacity for divergent thinking deteriorates with age. Divergent thinking is about imagination. It is the ability to think about all of the possibilities. The main intervention that these children have is the traditional teaching, which tells them to be conscious about that one answer at the back of the book but they are told not to look and don't copy.

Between 1968 and 1985, George Land and Beth Jarman conducted an experiment with children. They originally designed it for testing potential NASA engineers and scientists on how innovative they were. The researchers asked 1,600 5-year-old children how many uses they could come up with for paperclips. They then retested those children at ages 10 and 15. And they tested a group of adults.

The results were shocking when we compare them to common beliefs about the intelligence of children vs. adults. The proportion of people who scored at the "Genius Level" on this test were:

Age group	Number of subjects	Year	% Of subjects scoring 'highly creative'
5 years	1,600 children	1968	98%
10 years	1,600 children	1973	30%
15 years	1,600 children	1978	12%
25+ years	2, 80,000 adults	1985	2%

Test results from the Land and Jarman study

What's truer is that young children do **divergent thinking** really well. They don't yet have those voices inside their heads that remind them that their dozens of ideas are silly or stupid. So, they do their divergent thinking first. Then, after experimenting with it, they do their **convergent thinking** (Convergent thinking is about discernment and choice making. From all of the possibilities, which might be the best choice?)

A War in the Brain

As people grow up, Land's research shows that what actually happens is that a war begins to happen in the brain. Divergent and convergent thinking happens in 2 different parts of the brain. The older people get, the more likely that instead of convergent thinking happening after divergent thinking, divergent and convergent thinking are trying to happen at the same time.

The divergent part of the brain starts to fire. It would like to be as imaginative as that 5-year-old and is bursting with ideas. The convergent part of the brain immediately leaps into action and begins to filter those ideas, discarding all the "dumb" ones before they are even fully thought through or expressed. It's a protective mechanism from all the education people have received that has focused on finding the "right" answer as fast as possible and the repercussions if you don't. Probably the affective filter sets in.

How does this matter in English?

Divergent thinking is critical for language competency. It is important to focus on "What to say?" rather than "What is the correct way to say it?". Asking for all of the possible ideas, rather than the best ideas. Using the ideas which are gathered subconsciously through observation of the surroundings is more important than the conscious formulation. We must celebrate mistakes and failures with the same joy as you celebrate success.

3. The Freedom of Making Mistakes

Let us consider the same example, a child eventually starts recognizing his mother with the word "mama". One day the baby finally says "mama". Maybe with the wrong pronunciation. Do the parents immediately check his wrong pronunciation? Do they start teaching him grammar? Certainly not.

On the contrary, everyone is smiling, appreciating, and loving the baby for attempting to speak a word (even with bad pronunciation). Speaking English becomes a happy time for the baby. We find listening to a 1-year-old talk so delightful. Their initial sentences may be full of inappropriate vocabulary, fuzzy logic, and grammar violations.

When a 1-year-old points to a dog and says *"meow,"* we find it so cute. When a child says, *"I goed park today,"* we don't insult the child. We instead correct her by gently saying, *"No Sunny, not goed. Went!"*. Are we that kind to adults? We're even worse to ourselves.

Mistakes? They are bad. As we learn in school, we make a mistake, the teacher immediately corrects us. Making mistakes means lower test scores, we dreaded making them. And we carry over this fear when we're learning English as adults.

That's the reason why unless we're 100% sure of its correctness, we don't want to utter a single sentence in English. First, we check that the words are in their proper order, the verbs are in the proper tense, and agree with the subject in number and gender.

Now, why do you think, a 10-month-old has no problems committing more mistakes in one sentence than she has words? Because she wouldn't even know that something's wrong. She just grows up and continues to focus on *listening. Her speech will become gradually better. She will use more words. Her grammar will improve even without studying grammar rules. Her pronunciation will improve.*

This is the natural way of learning English. Your English did not improve like this probably because you didn't learn like this. For you, English was not a joyful experience. It was not a natural or playful experience that you may love.

Why don't we duplicate this spirit of a child?

As an English learner, you need to be comfortable with making mistakes. Make hundreds and thousands of mistakes. As James Joyce said, *"Mistakes are the portals to discovery"*.

Make a mistake while speaking naturally and laugh along the way. Maintain a playful attitude. Be flexible. Have fun. Enjoy the process of learning. It is important to speak like a human being. No one wants to speak to be in a conversation with a robot. Learn from your mistakes and if you're as diligent in correcting those mistakes as you are in making them, soon you will be able to speak English fluently and fearlessly.

4. The pleasure of Repetition

I remember when my daughter was 1-2 years old, she couldn't get enough of those rhythmic rhymes. Or while watching her favorite cartoon musical on YouTube, she wanted me to keep rewinding and playing multiple times. I wondered; will she ever get bored of it?

But to my surprise, each time was like the first time. She wasn't getting sick of it. In fact, it was getting more exciting and fun for her.

Research done in Britain finds that repetition of reading and speaking activities in second language instruction is effective in promoting greater language fluency and larger active vocabularies. Giving students a chance to repeat an activity gives them more chances to succeed and excel.

Repetition is an essential part of learning all kinds of skills. When you learn to play guitar, you play the same notes end several times until you master it. While playing cricket you practice a single shot multiple times in order to gain perfection. Language is also a skill and to master it, you need to repeat things over and over again.

One major reason why babies learn so fast, it's because they learn things over and over—to the point of overlearning. As adults, we lack the patience to overlearn a lesson, we are unable to repeat the same lesson time and again. We will start feeling bored and exhausted. We find ourselves "stuck." This lack of progression is instantly followed by the feeling that time is being wasted. We cannot control the urge of moving quickly on to the next lesson. When we do this, it harms and slows down our learning.

We may repeat a vocabulary word 3 to 5 times and expect it to stay with us for life—believing it will now be saved in our long-term memory. Do you think it's possible?? Unless you're a genius with an eidetic memory, repetition will be one of your saviors in the journey of English mastery.

Repetition might be in the form of replaying videos, rereading words, rewriting vocabulary, re-listening to podcasts, and re-doing games and exercises. Keep on repeating it until it becomes a habit. Remember, "Use it or lose it"

5. The Importance of Immersion

Imagine, what will you experience, if you are an Indian, who has never heard or spoken English? All of a sudden you find yourself in the middle of America with no access to the internet. Everything is new. You will try your best to use your innate abilities to make generalizations, read the context, listen to native speakers, and imitate how they speak. Everything is aligned. You would require to learn how to communicate fast, otherwise, you won't get to eat—even when you're sitting in a restaurant. This experience is a totally immersive experience where you're not learning a language just for grooming yourself or for improving your resume. You're doing it for your very survival. (That takes care of the "motivation" part of your learning.)

Children learn a language like this. It's a totally immersive and authentic experience—all their early language lessons are learned in a meaningful social context. Have you ever met a baby who learned his first language by enrolling in a class? And is there anything more immersive than a baby being born and experiencing the world by observation?

Immersion can actually train your brain to process information similar to the natives. Numerous studies show that students who are exposed to the language they are learning in an immersive way, be it through a bilingual immersion program or a study-abroad experience. They exhibit higher levels of fluency), particularly when the motivation to learn and absorb the language is high. The high motivation, in turn, is fostered by the desire to belong to or approximate the culture of the target language. We are wired to desire emotional and social connection, and when placed in contexts where such connection is only available through a foreign language, our motivation to acquire it increases.

For the adult language learner, experiencing immersion can be rare. One way of achieving immersion is to listen to as much English as possible. In later chapters we have discussed, 'What should you listen to?' And to practice active listening that gives you a complete immersion.

The human brain is an incredible Language learning machine. Humans are designed to learn languages. It is crystal clear that there is something wrong with conventional learning methods. For sure, we need some better strategies which could help us to learn English subconsciously. A natural process of learning (just like babies) that doesn't make English learning stressful and intimidating. With a natural approach to learning, you enjoy the process as you are not consciously fighting against nature or your brain.

"Adults are faster in attaining a second language proficiency than younger children."- Krashen

In the long run, those who start learning English as a child will usually be more competent than those who start as adults. In the short run, adults attain English mastery faster than younger children. Let us understand the reasons for the same.

1. More comprehensible input

The initial rate of Language acquisition is higher in adults as they have a higher understanding of the language than a child. The research was conducted by Scarcella & Higa, which studied children, aged 8.5 and 9.5 years and adolescents ages 15.5 and 16.5 who were engaged in a block-building task with the native speakers of English. They reported that although the younger acquirers received a comparatively simpler input, the older acquires were able to keep the conversation going and were able to modify the input. So the ability to build the conversation may actually help the older acquirer to get more comprehensible input (chapter 5) which in turn is responsible for their greater speed of language acquisition.

2. Greater knowledge of the world

Imagine a child of eight years and an adult of 28 years. The same message is delivered to both of them. The linguistic competence will be much more comprehensible to the adult owing to the greater amount of background information and experience. Older acquirers have a greater and wider knowledge of the world. This gives them an extra edge to help make the input comprehensible.

The children turn out to be better acquirers of English due to the affective factors. They possess the right attitude- high motivation, self-confidence, and low anxiety.

Did you know, we could get inspired by little kids so much about learning a foreign language? If you follow these five ways, the path that the babies have laid out for you, (1) Listen, (2) use the power of imagination, (3) don't be afraid to make mistakes, (4) repeat everything, and (5) immerse yourself in your target language. And keep a cheerful and playful attitude towards English like the babies, then whether it's French, Spanish, Japanese, Korean, Russian, or English you'll be speaking any target language like the natives-fearlessly, effortlessly, and subconsciously.

CHAPTER SEVEN

The 3 Heroes or The 3 Villains - Grammar, Vocabulary, and Pronunciation

What are the 3 things that come to your mind whenever you think of learning and speaking English impactfully? Of course, the 3 masters, the 3 heroes, and the 3 pillars of English- **Grammar, Vocabulary & Pronunciation.** In chapter 3, we understood the importance of vocabulary over Grammar. It is important to have a good command of vocabulary for effective communication. Grammar is equally significant. The basic study of the set of grammar rules helps you to create proper sentences and weave sentences to build up a conversation.

Imagine if vocabulary words are the building blocks, and grammar offers the glue and the nails which put the structure together. So Basic grammar knowledge for any language proficiency is essential.

In this chapter, we are going to discuss the 3rd pillar of English- Pronunciation. It is a recognized scientific fact that a child born in any country of the world can learn to speak any language on our planet. For example, a child has come to live in the USA, from India, at an early age. He or she will speak perfect English and have no Indian accent. His linguistic competency will not depend on grammar study or the list of words taught to him in school. And of course, such children will perfectly understand everything they hear, and other English speakers understand them.

Pronunciation and a clear understanding of English speech are two skills that complement each other. It means that the knowledge to pronounce the words and phrases correctly, with proper intonation, will automatically increase your level of speech understanding. Improving your pronunciation can help you learn English more easily. This is because pronunciation forces you to listen to speakers more carefully, focusing on how they make the right sounds when they speak. By listening to how natural sentences sound, you are more likely to make them yourself. Besides, the more you listen to these sentences, the easier it becomes for you to understand and get used to them.

Why is pronunciation Important?

Pronouncing the words correctly is an important factor for English fluency. when you pronounce the word incorrectly, it drags the attention of the listener immediately. If your pronunciation is improper, other people may have trouble understanding you even if you express your ideas logically and coherently. Pronunciation of the letter sounds in words as well as syllable emphasis on parts of words will more often than not change the meaning and context of the word drastically thereby irreversibly altering the meaning of the sentence being communicated. For instance, using the word 'present'. If one were to mention "I am present" with stress on the first syllable of the word, one is pertaining to one's presence at a specific place or time. On the other hand, if one were to say "I wish to present...." Then one refers to a statement or article one wishes to share.

Imagine a situation where a student's grammar and vocabulary are exceptionally good, he or she may be able to write good English. But, if that same student lacks fundamental knowledge of pronunciation despite having an excellent knowledge of grammar, etc. his or her English communication skills will be incompetent. He or she will be able to write in English, but will not be able to construct a meaningful sentence when speaking, resulting in a failure in communicating a message.

In case you feel that your English speaking is more influenced by your native tongue, you definitely need to work on this. Pronunciation is all about making sure you sound clear and are easy to understand.

By using the correct sounds when you speak, others can quickly understand what you're trying to say. If you're great at grammar and know various words, good pronunciation will help others hear and understand you even more clearly. Don't let your pronunciation stop you from feeling confident in your speaking skills

Don't miss the forest for the trees

You understand that Grammar, Vocabulary, and Pronunciation are an integral and most significant part of language learning. Especially when the language is English. But don't you think these heroes of English transform into villains in the journey of language learning when the path you follow is the conventional learning method. When something has a negative influence over any aspect of your life, you're giving it power over you - and that can hold you back. Any time you allow something to have an adverse impact on the way you think, feel, or behave, you give it the power to rule over your mind and body.

There is a saying in English "Don't miss the forest for the trees." To explain, if you concentrate only on two trees in a big forest, for sure you are going to miss the beauty of that exotic forest. If your entire focus is on these 3 villains of English you will miss the bigger picture. And what is the bigger picture in the case of

English speaking? The bigger picture is- fluent and confident communication in English. While speaking in English with someone we concentrate too much on the structuring of sentences, subject-verb agreement, tenses, prepositions, and so on and so forth. Sometimes we are busy incorporating fancy words, idiomatic expressions, and phrases in our speech in our talk so much so that we miss out on the essence, the ideas, the thoughts, and the logical order which we are going to share with the people.

The next thing which acts as a hurdle in our fluent English speaking is pronunciation. We try to use the dictionary or google pronunciation in our speech. That is what we have been taught as English learners through the textbooks in the traditional classes. Pronunciation and intonation go hand in hand. We need to enjoy the English language in a musical way. Like music, every language has its rhythm and melody. The speed and the stress constitute the rhythm and the intonation, the enunciation, constitutes the melody. The intonation is the rise and fall of the voice, the volume, and the speed of the speaker which makes speaking expressive and can help a person to understand the emotions behind your words.

Because we pay too much heed to these villains, we miss out on our chance to develop our listening, speaking, and communication skills. "Remember you don't build muscles while fighting in the ring." That is done much before while practicing. When a boxer is in the ring, he isn't calculative in applying his techniques, jabs, hooks, and punches. The process is natural and automatic. The process of learning and acquiring English should be such, that you can speak English subconsciously without any conscious effort.

Human focus is limited

In 2016, research was made at the Linkoping University, Linkoping, Sweden. Research finds, that the human brain is really clever and helps us concentrate on what we need to do. But the brain can't cope with too many tasks at one time. Only one sense at a time can perform at its peak.

Imagine someone speaking to you in English and you need to answer or respond. As soon as you listen to those English words your mind gets busy translating those words into your native language to decode and understand the message. Then it is busy translating the answer from your native language to English, applying all the grammar rules you have studied, present continuous, future perfect, conjugations, articles, prepositions, trying to recall vocabulary words from your vocabulary list, using the word-to-word pronunciation. So much to do.

"A higher cognitive load impairs the brain's response to sound not only in the auditory cortex but also in the parts of the brain that deal with emotions." The results of the research state that the brain activity in the cortex continues without any problems as long as we are subject to sound alone. So, if we concentrate on how to understand the message, and how to form the answer rather than understanding what is the message, we will not be able to communicate effectively and powerfully.

"Focussing on What is being said is more important than How it is being said."

Human focus is limited, it can consciously focus on one thing at a time. Either translations, rules, vocabulary, pronunciation, or listening to what is being said. One of these has to be subconscious.

So don't let these 3 heroes of the English Language become the villains for your English-speaking skills. If we pay attention to them, we empower them to take the most important decisions of our life, allow them to impact us, influence us and trick our minds to think that we can actually fail. Take the reins of your speaking in your hands. Don't let your conscious brain rule over your imagination and creativity. Feel free and let these heroes work silently and subconsciously.

CHAPTER EIGHT

The Tyranny of Grammar-Analysis Paralysis

The grammar mindset rules the society

The other day a parent approached me and said, "mam, I want to enroll my child in English-speaking classes." I asked, "why do you want your child to learn English speaking? Your child is studying in an English medium school, he has spent more than 6 to 8 years in that school. He understands English well. The only thing is he doesn't want to speak, which is due to certain fears. It doesn't mean he can't speak in English." He said, "ma'am I want to make him learn from the scratch." I asked, "what is the definition of "from the scratch?" he replied, "I want to make him learn Grammar." The Grammar mindset rules, the society.

The mindset has its roots in the fact that we fear making even a single grammatical mistake while speaking in English. We feel we will become a piece of mockery, especially by the grammar Nazis of society. However, this doesn't happen with us while speaking in our native language. Even if we make a mistake, we just laugh it off. Then why are we so conscious of English?

Preparation kills the conversation

How many times have you come across a situation, when you are just thinking a lot about –'How to say something in English?' But actually, you can say absolutely nothing. All the grammar tenses, verbs, conjugations, words, and phrases are flustering your mind and the information overload blocks your functional memory.

You may have never given it specific attention, but the major cause of this problem is the preparation while responding. Whenever we have to say something in English, instead of speaking it aloud spontaneously, we end up preparing our speech in our conscious mind. What happens is, that the more time you take to think about how to respond or how to say something in English, the more options you have to choose from. There is information overload and as a result the cognitive load increases.

Following this, you suffer from three things

1. Lack of quick decision making
2. Fear of making mistakes and
3. Perfection paralysis

Let us understand, **WHY** is this happening and find a solution to it.

1. Lack of quick decision making

Imagine all your English knowledge and skill inside a box. Now, you come across an English speaker and you have to respond. Can you process all that information and knowledge instantly and produce fluent English speech? Certainly not!

Every human being has natural limitations and can process a limited amount of information at a time. This is when 'information overload occurs. The reason why your speech becomes broken and hesitant is that your brain has to make multiple decisions within a millisecond. Before you create a sentence in English you have to decide, what grammar tense you should use, and immediately the grammar tenses table will flash in front of your eyes.

For example, you go to a restaurant with your friend, the night before, which was known to you. So, you might think it happened before a certain moment in past, so I must use past perfect tense in which we use *had* along with the *past participle form of the main verb* – "I had already been to the restaurant before where we ate last night............. where we were eating last night."

Hold on, I should use simple past or past continuous. No, past continuous would be inappropriate because I am not actually referring to the process of eating. I am talking about the place. So, I must use simple past tense.

Such kind of speech preparation and planning strategy must be going on in your brain and it's quite obvious that it distracts you from the real purpose, the main objective which is- SPEAKING.

So, your formal English knowledge and your textbook knowledge may be intense, still, this information overload causes you to lack quick decision making. You end up planning, analyzing, and predicting all the possibilities of 'what to say' and then trying to work out the best option among them all. Eventually, you find yourself struggling to produce fluent speech.

2. Fear of making mistakes

Imagine you are enthusiastically talking to someone but you hold it inside you because you are not sure you get it right. To make it even worse, you might even start avoiding conversations with people to avoid experiencing embarrassment and humiliation. The latter makes you even worse because no matter how badly you fear making mistakes your spoken English will not improve simply because you are not speaking enough.

So where does this fear of making mistakes come from? One of the major reasons is - information overload.

Remember in school, although we were encouraged to speak and express ourselves, at the same time our formal knowledge was constantly assessed and corrected against existing standards. As a result of which our focus shifted to upgrading our former textbook grammatical knowledge. This method works pretty well in exact & practical subjects such as Maths and Science, where we need to memorize formulas and definitions to perform certain calculations thereby committing a mistake would lead us to a wrong answer.

But spoken English is not a subject. It is a skill, just like Arts and Music, where making a mistake helps you improvise. The small mistakes you make aren't as big as creating a real communication barrier. You are fine. *Spoken English is much more than just words.* It's about how you look at people. It's about your expressions, your emotions, your gestures, and your body language when you speak. Look at your mistakes as an integral part of being an English speaker. Just tell yourself making mistakes is normal and necessary, whenever you feel the onset of fear and anxiety while speaking.

But don't think I am professing to speak in bad & broken English, without any efforts to improve yourself. You definitely need to make your grammar right and also make use of proper words and phrases and so on. The point is to make you understand that you have to *ignore the fear of making mistakes* and don't allow it to become your communication barrier.

3. Perfection paralysis

When you know that there are many ways of saying the same thing, obviously you want to make sure you say it correctly and in the best possible way. That is quite natural and justified. But this urge for perfection leads to the analysis of your entire formal knowledge. You start analyzing all the information you have gathered over years and you fall prey to *perfection paralysis*

Imagine you're having a casual conversation with one of your colleagues and he asks you about your holiday plans. Now, you can simply say the first thing which strikes your mind, *"I am going for my holidays next month and this time we are going abroad"*. The other option is analyzing all the dos and don'ts of different ways of speaking about future actions. So, my holidays are planned, so it's confirmed that I will go maybe I should use the *will + verb in the future tense*. In this case, I will go for my holidays next month.

No, just a second, *will + verb future tense* is normally used when making instant decisions. Now my holidays are planned so I may use '*the going to' future tense* which is used for plans, so "*I am going to go for my holidays next month.*"

Oh wait, the whole thing has already been arranged so shouldn't I use *present progressive continuous tense*? – " *I am going for my holidays next month.*" Yes, that sounds like the best choice.

This entire analysis would surely not take anywhere near as long as it took you to read it. The purpose of sharing this was to make you understand how much work your brain has to put in and you speak English by overanalyzing things. In real life situation, it may take just a few seconds but anyhow it will damage your fluency and prevent you from speaking effortlessly and naturally.

So howto overcome such situations when your brain is suffering from information overload? What strategy to follow when you are caught in analysis paralysis? What is the solution?

1. Stop making calculated decisions

Understand when you are writing a speech in English on a piece of paper you have all the time in the world to think through all the grammar aspects. You can dedicate more time and resources to sculpting your English sentences to perfection. When you write, you can meet well-calculated decisions and decide what means of expression is the most suitable for the given situation.

But imagine while speaking to someone when you have already opened your mouth to say something and your partner is expectantly looking at you and you have all but a split of a second to make the decisions, your brain can't act that fast because you have a habit of choosing from the multiple choices and that's when you feel as if you are paralyzed and unable to deliver a normal speech. So, stop making calculated decisions. Be spontaneous in responding

2. Zip up your conscious brain

As we have discussed, speaking English is an art or skill. Just think about any other acquired skill you have- driving a car or playing an instrument or anything else that you are quite good at. Do you think about how to switch gears and when to switch from second to third gear while driving? If you would, your car would be jerking as a few drove it for the first time. Do you put conscious effort while playing piano, while pressing those white and black keys? Of course not! You don't or else you couldn't play in the rhythm

The commonality between the two actions is- automatic action. If you act automatically, you perform well as your conscious mind is not working. It's similar to talking with someone while driving. You don't pay any attention to the process of driving. Do you?

Your spoken English should be no different so just leave over analysis behind and zip up your conscious mind.

3. Communication over perfection

It is obvious that when you respond instantaneously and zip up your conscious analytical brain, you are bound to make some mistakes along the way. But then you need to understand that it's only going to get better and better over time. HOW?

When you engage in English conversation with other English speakers, your subconscious mind *acquires natural English speech patterns* used by others. So, your mistakes are minimized. You just need to have faith in yourself and stay motivated, because your thoughts and ideas are more important than perfection in your English.

It's important to accept that you are going to make more mistakes when speaking without analyzing but don't you think it's ok if it allows you to speak fluently and overcome your hesitation. So, accept your mistakes as natural and necessary.

4. Say the first thing on your mind

The best way to deal with all that information overload - the grammar tenses, conjugation, wordlists is to *just say the first thing on your mind.* Now, there are great chances that you might commit mistakes but as you get better you will realize that on most occasions the first thing that comes to your mind, isthe right thing to say. There might be times when that first thing is wrong. So what? Just go back and correct yourself or maybe just do nothing at all. Simply accept your mistake, and make a note of it so that you can rectify it in the future. Let me tell you if you make a mistake and reflect on it you remember it longer.

Speaking the first thing on your mind, doesn't mean that you go on rambling about anything that comes to your mind. By saying this I meant you need to stop making choices about *what to say.* However, you have to know *what you want to say.*

Sometimes getting stuck in the middle of the conversation is not due to information overload but it might be due to the fact that you simply don't have much knowledge or absolutely NO knowledge about the topic. So first you need to know what you want to say but then stop analyzing too much and just say something and enjoy the freedom of speaking subconsciously and effortlessly.

CHAPTER NINE

The Language of Parity & Prestige

People who speak English might find that they come across to others positively – for example, as being well-educated. For instance, it might be advantageous for a candidate in a job interview to speak fluently in English+, rather than in a regional or native language. While a job advertisement might not directly ask for a candidate with an English-speaking ability, this might be something that employers judge when selecting a suitable candidate from a group of possible employees. This preferential treatment makes the ability to speak in English an **overt prestige** for the users.

One of my students Rahul Halder says, "I belonged to an English medium school. When I completed my engineering, in every interview I appeared the first question thrown at me in every interview was- How good is your English? This made the entire interview experience intimidating. I became nervous and ended up spoiling everything that followed."

The other student Sahil Arora told, "After completing my B. Com honors, I appeared for an interview. Being a student of the regional medium throughout, I was not able to speak a single sentence in English. I appeared for one, two, three, and more than 30 interviews. Every time I faced criticism and humiliation due to my poor English speaking. My confidence was shattered and I made Fluent English the only mission of my life."

Traces from the history

Looking back into history, the British were given a lot of recognition and respect due to their political power, and they were required to adopt a pose that would fit their status. Language became a marker of the white man's power. Kachru quotes E. M. Forster in A Passage to India (Kachru 1986: 5):

"India likes gods. And Englishmen like posing as gods". The English language was part of the pose and power. Indians accepted it, too (ibid).

English was used in India and elsewhere in the colonies as a tool of power to cultivate a group of people who identify with the cultural and other norms of the political elite (cf. Macaulay's Minute). English was considered a "road to the light", a tool of "civilization". English provided a medium for understanding technology and scientific development.

In India, English gradually acquired socially and administratively the most dominant roles: the power and prestige of language were defined by the domains of language use. Ultimately the legal system, the national media, and important professions were conducted in English (Kachru 1986a: 7). In the words of Kachru, skilled professional Indians became the symbol of Westernization and modernization. English came to be used by Indians, as well. (Kachru 1986a:7).

By the 1920s English had become the language of political discourse, intranational administration, and law, a language associated with liberal thinking. Even after the colonial period ended, English maintained its power over local languages.

English today is considered a language of the elite. A language that earns power, recognition, and respect. It is proof of modernization and civilization.

A new caste system.

We are living in a nation where the majority, are unable to read the label of the medicine they need to give their child, the menu at a local restaurant, or even the warning signs on the road. It is a place where they are unable to comprehend the government documentation for filing their driver's license, tax filing, or marriage. Hundreds of millions of Indians live in this world simply because the elite prefers English.

The majority of people in India are considered illiterate and backward just because they lack knowledge of English. By not having medical instructions, food ingredient labels and nutritional information, government forms, access to the courts and politicians, street signs, and even movie tickets in their mother tongue, they are being wronged in the most biased way.

There is a system that marks this discrimination. The elite and middle classes send their children to English private schools while the majority of poor send their kids to the government schools which offer their mother tongue. However, it is understood that universities and even government jobs require fluency in English, as made compulsory by the ruling elite. Therefore, a person's socioeconomic status in Indian society is determined by his or her fluency in the language. This is a new caste system.

Inferiority Complex

"If you use poor English, whatever you say is discounted. If you use good English, the impression you make is profound- that impression cannot fail to win you a promotion, higher income, and ultimate success."

Ms. Seema Ravindran, a practicing Chartered Accountant, a state rank holder in +2, says, "I don't think English is a difficult language but whosoever speaks English is superior."

Academically Seema was a bright student. She was sent to a school where her native language was taught well. All her teachers were speaking in the native language. At home her mother although she was fluent in English, never spoke to her father or any other family member in English. Her cousins used to study at ICSE schools. She observed them mocking others when they made a mistake in speaking in English. So, she avoided communicating with them. She says," My cousin used to wear shoes, I wore sandals, they used to go to school by bus, I went walking. They willingly participated in their annual day celebrations, they participated in various competitions, and how they were willing to expose themselves. This confidence was due to their ability to speak English. This was something which created an inferiority complex in me and I became comfortably introverted."

"Even in college", she continues, "the fear of being mocked just because I was speaking in my native language created the fear of people in me" so being so talented and bright academically is not enough. You need a command of English to earn respect, recognition, and acceptance.

Held Back in Professional Growth

Let me share another experience, that I came across with Mr. Tahir Hasan- a podcaster, YouTuber, and communication skills trainer.

"Coming from a village, I was often mocked for my spellings, sentence construction, and speaking by my colleagues." Tahir says, "I always overheard everything and I would feel bad about it. But I used to think as long as I can understand the customer I can maintain my performance, as long as my manager is happy and I was getting top ratings, there is no need to work on my Speaking skills. I never realized that my English-speaking skills were one of my opportunity areas."

He was expecting a promotion- and that was vital to his success. The position required him to meet many other executives of his own and other firms, all educated men and he could hardly speak a sentence without making some crude and embarrassing mistake in English. His conversation was not polished enough to be a team leader.

He had been hoping for such a promotion, for years. As Tahir puts it, "I was given a responsibility to start a new business altogether and was told if I start the business well, the chances of my promotion will be high. One day, the manager's assistant asked me to follow him to the executive lounge. This was a place I had never been to. It was a big board meeting room. Many high-level officials were sitting in the room. He threw some questions at me. I was already intimidated because I had never spoken to people with such high authority in my life. I had the entire knowledge and capability to answer the questions, but I was not able to speak a single word. The mountain of my ignorance of English loomed before me. It gave me such a pronounced feeling of general inferiority in the presence of these executives that I finally decided to decline the offer. That was a life-defining moment for me. I accepted it as constructive criticism and started working on improving my English speaking."

Some men make the mistake of concentrating so intensely on becoming more efficient in their work that they neglect the development of their personality entirely. And speaking English naturally and effortlessly is one major aspect of a shining and magnetic personality.

The Panic Attack

English is inevitable when it comes to higher education. Ignorance of the English language can cause you to suffer from severe anxiety. May I tell you about a lady I know?

Dr. Anurita Surya is an MA, PGDCP, PGDRP & RCI Registered Psychologist. She belongs to a family which valued education. The native language of the family was Hindi. Her schooling was at a Hindi medium school. She entered the professional course with the fourth rank. Before she joined her professional course, she had never heard a single sentence in English, from any of her family members or her teachers. In her words, "The first day, when I attended the orientation class, I got to know that all the study material and medium of instruction would be English. For the first time, I heard the professor speaking in English. I thought, Oh My God! Definitely, I am going to fail! I didn't comprehend anything in the lecture. I was afraid of the professors, of my classmates. I got so conscious. I almost got a panic attack in the very first class."

She says," English will always follow you. There is no escape from English. Your education and professional journey are incomplete without English."

Humiliation

She further mentions," Although I was very accurate in my diagnosis, I was giving satisfactory results to my patients, I had a profound knowledge of my profession, some part of my life was missing. My juniors made fun of me, due to my poor English. They left no opportunity to pull me down or humiliate and ridicule me. I was under stress and then something happened which set a fire under me. And there was this burning desire to speak English fearlessly and powerfully."

"One day I had to present a case in front of other psychologists. Then my senior told me to present in English only. I told her ma'am my English is not good, please allow me to present in Hindi. She denied. She said English is so simple, just try. I tried. I fumbled. I spoke in broken English. I had to stop my presentation abruptly and had to exit the meeting awkwardly. I had done so much research and collected so much data. Everything was in vain. I cried and cursed myself for my poor English. My son is the witness to my multiple failures. He is the one who had consoled me every time. I have a vivid memory of these experiences whenever I share them."

Impression- Depression

I would also like to share the discussion with Mr, Shreyansh Ghosh, who works as an assistant manager and is an acting department head for international operations. He shares that he was born to a loving joint family and was brought up within a thick layer of comfort. Being a student of a Bengali medium school, he never realized the importance of learning English. He always believed in shortcuts. As he puts it, "I always had a fear, fear of failure, fear of getting judged if I go blank, if I fall short of words. Most of the time I feared that people will laugh at me. Someone is always watching me."

"My first job was in an international company. I fluked the interview somehow. When I went to the job and I was asked to give my introduction, my legs started shaking and I was shivering. The room was full of a mixed population. Being a student of the only boy's school, I had never faced girls. I never attended college too often as well. When I had to speak in front of the females, all my body parts were shaking. They wore difficult smiles. I could sense that. I was totally dumb and silent. Every day, in the office, was like a decade. I felt so nervous and jittery. Every day I went back home and shared my story with my father. Finally, after 3 months, I decided to quit. It was so frustrating and humiliating, that I can't begin to explain it to you. The only thing which helped me survive was my sound technical knowledge. But one day, after 3 months I finally decided to quit."

He says "Fluent English makes you sound intellectual and smart, no matter how good you are in your technical skills, good English is mandatory to fetch you respect at the workplace"

The stories related to bitter experiences with English are endless. As per a survey conducted by me, 96.1 % of people agreed that they suffer from nervousness, anxiety, and fear due to poor English skills.

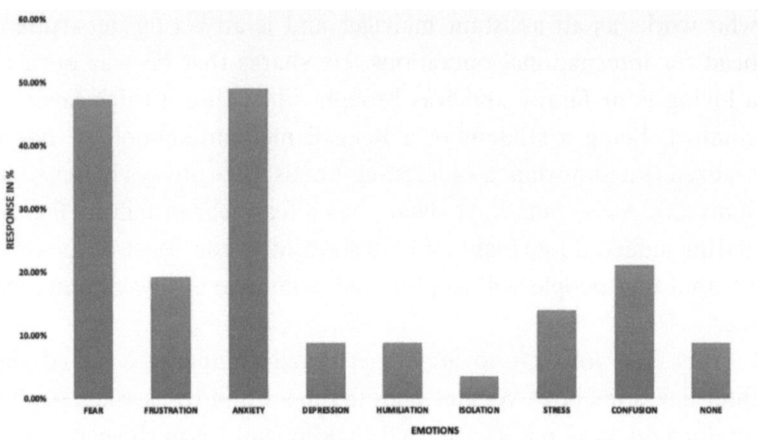

English & English Trauma

Why English has become the language of the elite?

Indians have come this far to trust that their country's success and their growth are entirely subject to not just learning English, in fact learning it as a first language. It started with the advent of the British, who made it the language of the elite, blasted inside the working class that was recruited by global organizations, and streamed to the vast majority, who want to get away from their desperation, however incapable to manage the cost of private English education.

Another survey shows, that only 30.8% of people believe that English is just a tool to convey your message. Others agree that it is a status symbol, it projects you as elite, it makes you sound more knowledgeable or educated, it makes you sound smart, it helps you make better friends, and it makes you a more aware human being.

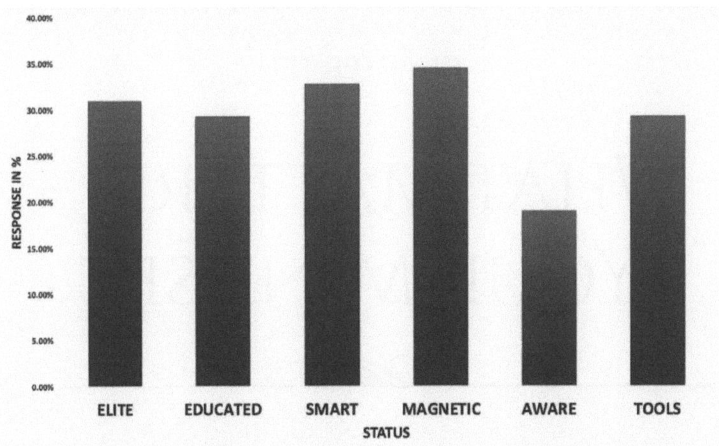

English & Prestige issue

There are so many emotional stories, that tell us how people have suffered "The English Trauma" in their lives. In the coming chapters, we will understand the mindset and strategies that will help us to overcome "The English Trauma."

CHAPTER TEN

WHAT MATTERS? - YOUR MINDSET

"I fear making mistakes and I am always searching for that one right answer, I feel stressed and hopeless. I have spent so many years inside the English classrooms trying to learn and memorize grammar rules and vocabulary lists. Despite all this effort, I struggle with even the simplest of conversations with my husband and daughters in English." One of my students, Dr. Ridha Malik, told me this. She is a homeopathy practitioner, and a yoga trainer and had been in London, UK for over 25 years. When she came to me, she was so frustrated. She had suffered from English Trauma for so long, that she believed there was no solution.

"I cannot understand American TV shows or movies. I am unable to enjoy the movies and web series with my family. Howsoever good results I may give to my patients, I know they laugh at my poor English behind me." She was in pain. She was in tears while sharing this. She continues," My son-in-law doesn't understand Hindi. Whenever I want to speak with him, my daughter tells me to be quiet. She says, mom, you are embarrassing me with your broken English. My husband says you will be a bad English speaker till your grave. When I see them losing patience, I become even more nervous and make more mistakes."

Does this sound familiar? Even after putting in so many years of learning English through conventional methods, students still feel confused and stressed. While making conversations they cannot stop thinking about the grammar rules. The process they follow remains the same. Whenever they listen to something in English, they translate it into their native language, to understand what is being said. They translate their response from native to English, apply grammar rules to assure that the response is correct, and then finally speak. Thus, making their speech unnatural and hesitant. This long process makes English feel so boring and difficult. Natural English speakers are fast, there is no time for all this thinking while in a real-life conversation.

When you engage yourself in translations and grammar rules while in a conversation with an English speaker, you will lose track. Instead of listening to what the person is saying, you will be busy translating and remembering grammar. Human focus is limited, remember we discussed in chapter 7. Soon you become confused your speech becomes hesitant and broken. The other person may become frustrated with your inability to understand and when you see the other person losing patience you may become nervous. This creates a vicious downward spiral.

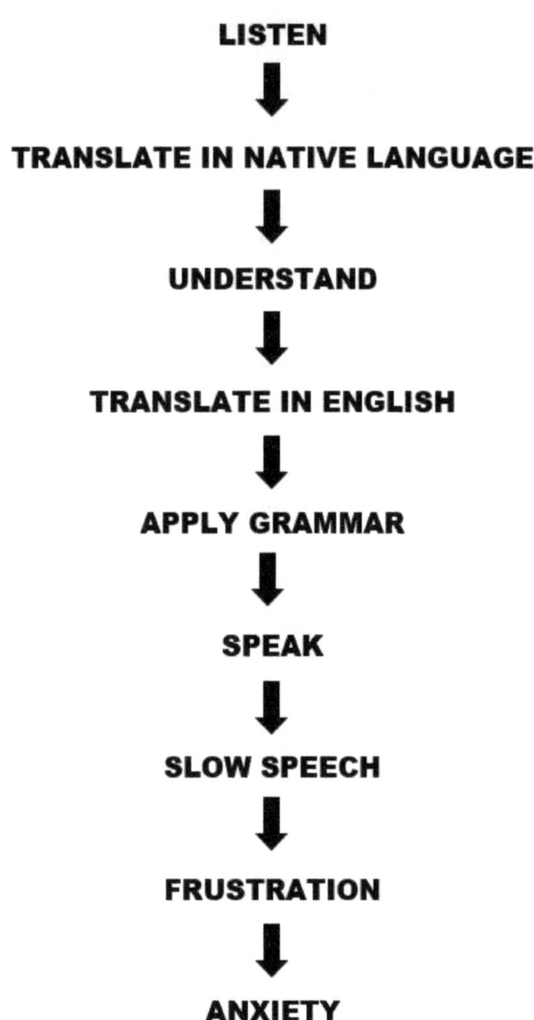

The Downward Spiral

So, what is the solution to this vicious downward spiral? How can you speak English, naturally, powerfully, clearly, impactfully, fluently, and fearlessly? How can you speak English without any conscious effort? How can you speak English subconsciously?

The solution comprises of two things:

1. The Mindset (Correct Psychology)
2. The Skillset (Turbo English Mastery Program)

For this, you need to change your beliefs about English and unlearn the way you have been learning English.

Schools only focus on the parts of language- grammar & vocabulary. English speaking has nothing to do with grammar. Grammar is only important in schools as a subject just like science or maths. Wherein you need to fill in the correct answer according to the rules to score good marks on the test. Grammar is a set of rules which will not help you in communication improvement as we discussed in chapter 8. The traditional methods ignore the most important part of language learning- Psychology. When you think of your English speaking, the major problems you struggle with are nervousness, frustration, and lack of confidence. What is the solution to these problems?

You can have the best resources in the world, but if you are not in the right frame of mind to engage with the new language and use the opportunities before you, then you are unlikely to do so.

According to a research paper, by the Department of Applied Linguistics and Communication, University of London, London, United Kingdom, "For many years, a cognitive perspective had dominated research in applied linguistics. Around the turn of the millennium, researchers became increasingly interested in the role of emotions in foreign language learning and teaching, beyond established concepts like foreign language anxiety and constructs like motivation and attitudes toward the foreign language."

Mindset

In chapter 4 we understood English speaking is an art, it is a skill that can be acquired as implicit knowledge. Understand, any skill is 80% Psychology and 20% Habits. What is Psychology? It is our mindset. The set of thoughts that we hold in our mind. **'It's all in the mind!'** – This is so true when it comes to learning a foreign language.

Skill = 80% Mindset + 20% Habits

Your Success depends upon your Beliefs

Your mindset depends on your beliefs. Beliefs are the assumptions or the perceptions we hold in our minds. For example, God is a belief. You may believe in God. You may not Believe in God. Your beliefs affect every aspect of your life, be it professional or personal. They may affect your health, relationships, your growth in business, and even your communication skills. We build beliefs through observations and experiences. It can be parents, friends, society, the education system, media, television, or movies. We just observe them and unconsciously build beliefs. The fact we are not acquiring them consciously we accept them blindly, without checking or validating them. When these beliefs are based on some facts or statistics, they are good. But if the beliefs are not realistic, they are not supported by any facts, they will result in frustration, failure, stress, and sometimes anxiety too.

So, the problem is associated with mindset. Your mentality is more important than your ability. If you want to be a good English speaker you need the correct mindset. Correct psychology will help you speak English confidently and fearlessly.

Brain Re-Programming

Our beliefs guide our decisions, feelings, behavior, and even thoughts. They decide our abilities and weaknesses. They help us to achieve success, they are responsible for our failures. The beliefs can be divided into two broad categories: limiting beliefs and empowering beliefs.

Limiting beliefs to Empowering Beliefs

The limiting beliefs are the wrong beliefs that we are holding. They are false, illogical, and irrational. They limit your potential and performance. To put it correctly, they limit your success. The traditional methods of English teaching are responsible for the negative programming of the brain of the students with limiting beliefs. Our beliefs determine our behavior. Our thoughts and feelings depend upon our beliefs.

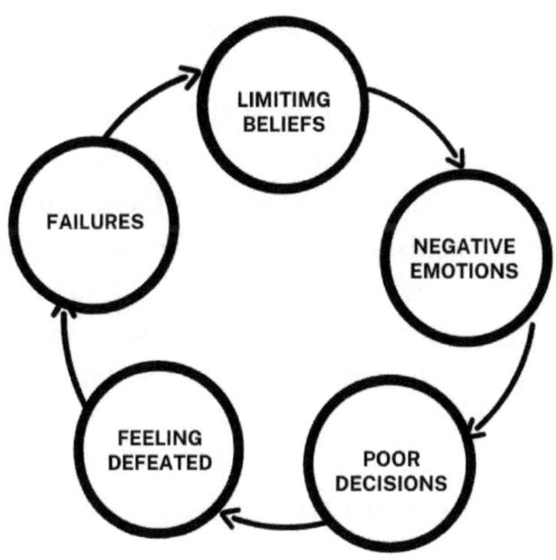

The Vicious circle of Limiting Beliefs

Here are a few negative beliefs and the kind of behavior you develop with those beliefs and how we can reprogram our brains by changing them into realistic empowering beliefs?

1. Grammar study will make me fluent.

The grammar Nazis will completely disagree with me. Grammar study is important for giving tests in school. Grammar should be developed naturally not through grammar drills. This belief comes from schools, to develop anything we need to follow rules. It is true in the case of Science and Maths, but not English. The children who belong to convent schools speak fluent English not because they have studied grammar well but because they were immersed in English. Those who are from vernacular are unable to speak smoothly even after having grammar in their curriculum, because of the absence of an English-speaking environment. The people who possess this belief will always be worried about making mistakes. They always feel stressed. They will speak synthetic and robotic English. They may be good at written English but their spoken English will remain slow and hesitant.

The way to change this negative belief into an empowering belief is, by telling yourself, "Even if I have never been to school, I can speak fluent English." Take an example of any country where the native language is English. There must be many people who have never gone to school, but still, they can speak fluent English. They haven't learned grammar in school. They have **acquired it naturally and subconsciously**. How to do that? We will learn in the coming chapters.

2. There are shortcuts to English

When you assume that the English learning process is quick and you can master it instantly without putting in hours of practice and commitment, you are mistaken. Where does this mindset come from? Obviously, the various you-tube videos, which offer you tips tricks, and strategies to master English in a few days. Tell me, did you acquire your native language in just 21 days?

If you want to master English you need to practice every day. Consider any other skill, dancing, singing, swimming or even playing cricket. Everything requires patience, repetition, lengthy process. You have to develop your HFT- High Frustration

Tolerance. You have to accept the reality. Imagine how many hours of hard work and practice those seasoned singers, dancers, actors, footballers, or cricketers put in to become as good as they are before they go on stage or field. **"When you practice in private, you are rewarded in public."** You need to be disciplined; you need to put in daily practice to achieve fluency just like your native language. English learning is a journey. You need to be a lifelong learner. Keep learning. Keep practicing. Keep performing.

3. Fluency can be achieved by practicing a few minutes daily.

Do you also carry this belief? What can you do in just 15 -20 minutes or maybe one hour? Language is a blend of 4 skills-listening, speaking, reading & writing. Can you do all 4 in just an hour? You may be solving the grammar exercises for one hour and expect your English to improve. You may be reading a newspaper or watching a YouTube video for an hour. You will not improve your English this way. You may end up getting frustrated and quitting after a month or two.

How can you change this belief? The only way to learn a language is to *immerse your brain in the language.* You need to submerge your brain in English surroundings. A language cannot be memorized. Language comes naturally, it flows naturally. It will flow only when you develop English habits. Change your beliefs. Spend more hours of practice. Three, Five, Eight hours, the more the better. When you practice for long hours, you develop the courage and the fearless attitude that helps you to speak English subconsciously.

4. I should speak perfect English.

There is nothing as perfection. There is not just one right answer and one right way of saying it. You can express yourself in several ways. The moment you think about speaking perfect English you fall into perfection paralysis. You will constantly end up thinking about perfection. You will keep on analyzing your grammar while speaking. You will always feel stressed and frustrated because all you can think about is your mistakes. You will keep on checking in your head. You will always be concerned with the listener's reaction. You will constantly think, "Have I said something wrong? Are they laughing at me?" when you speak with some more authoritative person or a fluent English speaker you will instantly switch to your native language. The reason is you think, that if I will make a mistake while speaking in English, they might judge me, mock me or think I am not smart enough.

How to change this mindset? Just believe, there is nothing perfect in nature. "*Just express don't impress.*" Focus on expressing your ideas, thoughts, and suggestions people want to communicate with you for your ideas and thoughts, not for your perfect English.

5. No one should laugh at my English

When you carry this mindset, you either don't try at all or if you speak and someone laughs at you, you get hurt. You can't control other people's behavior. People will laugh, you can't dictate them not to laugh. They will judge you. It's their habit. We can't change that.

What you can control is your behavior, you can *choose your response*. It's you who has to decide, whether you want to try, speak, and improve or whether you want to stay quiet because people are laughing at you. When you are least bothered about people's reactions, you become confident and fearless. In other words, "Be Shameless."

6. Fluency reflects intelligence

When you come across fluent English speakers, you get nervous and try to avoid that person. You think they are more intelligent than you.

Understand *English is just a language, knowledge depends on a multitude of factors*. If English could make a person intelligent all the native speakers would have been scholars. When you change your belief, you speak confidently and fluently.

Mentioned below are a few other examples of limiting beliefs and behavior developed due to them. I have also tried to mention a way how you can train your brain and replace them with a positive and 'Empowering belief"

No.	Limiting belief	Behaviour	Empowering Belief
1	English is difficult & complicated	You may struggle with forced learning. You will be demotivated and English will be stressful for you.	English is easy, fun, interesting & exciting
2	Only a few special people can master English.	You become frustrated quickly, you may "I am a bad learner", or "There is some problem with me." There will be slow progress.	Anyone can learn to speak English powerfully.
3	I make a lot of mistakes.	You will be conscious of your grammar and will not be able to focus on the context. Your English will be artificial	Mistakes are normal and necessary. Even native speakers make mistakes.
4	My test scores are low; thus, I can't speak fluent English.	You will always be looking for one correct answer to score more marks on tests, rather than focussing on creativity and imagination.	Communication, not the test score, is the purpose of English speaking.
5	Something is wrong with me because I still can't speak English fluently	You become frustrated with your methods and end up quitting everything. Obviously, the methods you are using are not working.	There's nothing wrong with me. I've been using a bad method. I must change it.

Negative beliefs are the central programs in our brain that create feelings, decisions, and emotions. Beliefs are based on your experiences. Every time you have an experience your brain decodes it into a meaning which is remembered by your brain for your entire life. Each negative experience makes your negative beliefs stronger and stronger. Eventually, you become absolutely certain about that belief.

For example, maybe someone made fun of you for your wrong English. Someone corrected you for your wrong grammar. Your brain decodes each of these embarrassing experiences for you to understand that you are a bad English speaker. Your brain indicates that English is painful and humiliating. Each negative experience will make your belief stronger.

These negative beliefs will affect all the English experiences which follow thereafter. So, whenever you will have to speak English, these negative mindsets will always harm your speaking, making you more conscious and nervous. Imagine if you don't train your brain to change these limiting beliefs, one day your ability to become a fluent English speaker will be destroyed. So, you must replace your limiting beliefs with positive empowering beliefs, that give you the power to propel you as a confident and fluent speaker. Every time you have a negative thought, just replace it with a positive strong thought as mentioned in all the points above.

How to Re-program your brain?

Empowering beliefs are strong beliefs. They create a feeling of confidence and excitement. So, they are more desirable. What can we do to create this positive attitude towards English?

1. Modeling

Modeling is one of the techniques which help you to***reach the excellence that the best people have reached.*** With modeling, you need to study and follow the extraordinary results of successful people by mirroring their conscious and unconscious behavior. The principle and idea behind modeling are that if you follow the behaviors, strategies, beliefs, language (words, phrases, questions), emotional states, and other traits of successful people, you will also become more successful.

If you want to speak English powerfully, for example, you need to find the other person who learned to do it. Learn about them. Learn what they did, and how they did it? Once you have access to someone who has achieved the fluency you wish to achieve you could simply ask them, "Teach me how to do that!" Talk to them, and learn about their psychology and methods. Try to do your best to do exactly what they did.

Modeling others comes naturally to human beings. For example, A child doesn't pay as much attention to what his parents say or command, he does what they do. The more you model successful people, the more your beliefs change automatically. By shifting your mindset from failures to success, you are gradually reprogramming your brain.

It is quite possible you are unable to find **your role models, you're still influenced by the people who surround you.** It's said that "you are the average of the 5 people you spend the most time with." You acquire the mindset, psychology, behavior, values, beliefs, and actions of the people you spend the most time with. You are subconsciously modeling them. Slowly you acquire their attitude and behaviors.

This is exactly what I did when I created the Turbo English Mastery Program. I studied most of the successful English learners. I interviewed them. I studied their psychology, their emotions, and their learning strategies. This is the reason my system is based on success psychology.

2. Selective memory

We discussed that our beliefs are created by our observations and experiences. The human brain is conditioned to focus more on negative experiences. According to research," People should exhibit a greater than normal tendency to selectively process the self-depreciatory rather than the self-appreciatory information." The more you focus on negative experiences, the stronger our limiting beliefs become. The trick is, that you can make your empowering beliefs stronger in a similar way- by using “selective memory”.

For this follow the following steps:

- Review all your past experiences with English.
- Search for any experiences that were positive. For example, reading a short story in English to your child, reciting an English poem in class, or giving an English speech, where you were appreciated and applauded by the people. You will definitely find a lot of such experiences. Research says, “The accuracy of people’s memories for personality feedback depends on their level of self-esteem and the favourability of that feedback. Participants remembered feedback more accurately when the affectability of that feedback was congruent with their self-esteem.”
- Write them down
- Create a list of all the positive experiences and stick it at a place where you can see it easily every day.
- Focus your attention on those memories
- Review your list daily.
- Recall each experience, and feel the positive experience again.
- Every day add an empowering belief to the list.
- Review each day. Keep on adding any positive experience you come across.
- Let the list become longer and longer.
- Let your empowering beliefs grow stronger.

Positive beliefs create an upward spiral that helps you to become a confident and fearless English speaker.

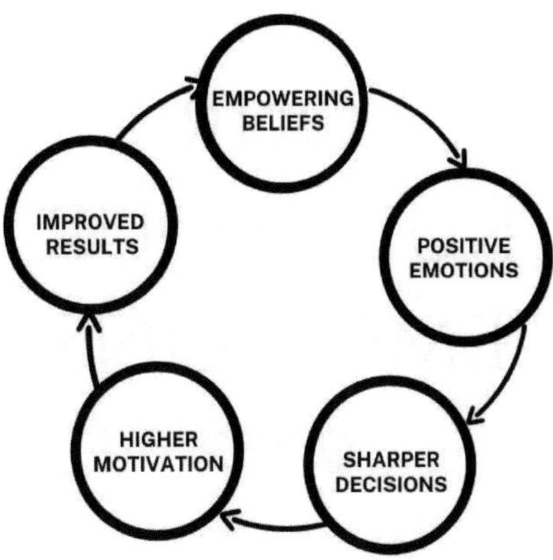

This upward spiral is the secret recipe to rapid success in English.

CHAPTER ELEVEN

TRAIN YOUR BRAIN-RULE YOUR EMOTIONS

Imagine you are on a road to English fluency and you are in the driver's seat. Let us consider different scenarios

1. Old slow car + cheap fuel

Your ride will be slow. There will be frequent breakdowns. You may get frustrated and give up after a few miles. You won't be able to reach your destination at all.

1. Old slow car + high-quality fuel

You may start up with energy. It may help you to reach a bit far. Still, you will take longer than expected.

3. Formula 1 Racing car + low-quality fuel

Your ride will be faster than the old car. But after a few miles, your car will start encountering problems because racing cars require high-quality fuel. You may end up stopping abruptly in the middle of your journey.

4. Racing car + high-quality fuel

Your journey will be fast, exciting, and energetic. You will be supercharged and thrilled to reach your destination and you will reach there much faster.

You have tried to learn English through various sources-websites, YouTube videos, books, private classes, and online learning courses. All these are different types of cars to reach your destination – fluent and fearless English. But remember, even the fastest and most advanced car will not be able to carry you to your destination if you don't fill it with the best quality fuel. And the best quality fuel is – your *positive psychology.*

Positive Psychology

As identified by Seligman and Csikszentmihalyi (2014), "positive psychology is based on the pillars of positive institutions, positive personality characteristics, and positive experiences including emotions. These positive emotions and feelings and personality factors, along with empathy, enjoyment, happiness, contentment, optimism, tolerance, flow, love, and mindfulness, can result in a person's satisfaction, self-efficacy, and success."

Here they talk about 3 pillars

1. The Institutions

They are the practices and beliefs instilled by a community or society. For example, Grammar study is the key to fluency. This is a common belief fed by the society and education system. There are many more that we have discussed in chapter 10.

2. Personality characteristics

A study on Turkish University students, regarding the relationship of personality traits with English speaking Anxiety, found that extraversion, openness, and conscientiousness significantly and negatively but neuroticism and agreeableness significantly and positively predict foreign language speaking anxiety.

3. Experiences and emotions

There is a strong connection between English learning and emotions. If the process of your speaking English, is somehow connected to stress, fear, nervousness, and doubt, you will have a lot of problems. The various traditional methods which we discussed in chapter 2 are strong enough to create powerful negative emotions in the English learners.

As per an article published, titled, Researching and Practicing Positive Psychology in Second/Foreign Language Learning and Teaching: The Past, Current Status, and Future Directions, "By drawing on the broaden-and-build theory of positive emotions, we explain how individuals' positivity can result in their flourishment and development in any aspect of life, including L2 learning and teaching."

Role of Positive Emotions

You need to bring proper emotional energy to your language learning process. You need to have strong psychology, powerfully positive experiences of flow, hope, courage, well-being, optimism, creativity, happiness, grit, resilience, strengths, and laughter with the aim of enhancing your linguistic progress.

The *five functions* of positive emotions are as follows:

First, positive emotions tend to broaden people's attention and thinking, leading to exploration and play, new experiences, and new learning.

Second, positive emotion helps to undo the lingering effects of negative emotional arousal.

Third, the function of positive emotion is to promote resilience by triggering productive reactions to stressful events, such as improving cardiovascular recovery and making salient feelings of happiness and interest while under stress.

Fourth, positive emotion promotes building personal resources, such as social bonds built by smiles, and intellectual resources honed during creative play.

Fifth, positive emotions can be part of an upward spiral toward greater well-being in the future, essentially reversing the vicious downward spiral. (Chapter 10)

Most of the time the emotions that hit us whenever we think about English are, frustration, stress, boredom, exhaustion, fear, anxiety, nervousness, lack of confidence, and embarrassment. This hampers your learning. Remember 'the Affective Filter hypotheses of Dr, Stephen Krashen's Second Language Acquisition theory (chapter 5).

How to Rule Your Emotions through anchoring?

We need to control our emotions in order to expedite the process of language acquisition. This can be done through 'Anchoring'. "Anchoring bias is a process whereby people are influenced by specific information given before a judgment"- Department of Psychology, University of Bath, UK. Psychologists have found that people rely too much on the very first piece of information they learn, which can have a serious impact on the decision they end up making. In other words, anchoring bias connects your emotions to an experience or learning.

Positive Anchors

Positive anchors connect a positive experience to a positive emotion. For example, there might be a specific song from your childhood or your teenage or any phase of your life that you may have listened to, while you were feeling ecstatic, elated, or motivated. Now if that emotion was quite strong, a connection is formed between that song and your emotion. Every time you hear the song, and you are feeling good and happy, the connection will grow stronger.

Gradually, a strong connection is created between the song and the feeling of happiness. Probably, anytime you hear that song you will automatically feel a surge of happiness in yourself.

If you don't believe me, play your favorite song with which some happy experience is related, just close your eyes and observe a smile on your face. This is how positive anchors are created.

Negative Anchors

There can be negative anchors as well. To exemplify, there might be certain songs that may remind you of a painful incident or experience. In this case, the opposite of a positive anchor will be true. Every time you hear that song you will be reminded of that experience and your negative anchor will grow stronger. Similarly, you may have faced some humiliation or an embarrassing situation in an English class, where the teacher may have corrected you or ridiculed you for making a mistake in front of your classmates. Or your colleagues or friends may have mocked you for wrong pronunciation and this incident gets connected with your English learning experience.

How toControl the Emotions byReprogramming the Anchors?

A series of negative experiences may strengthen the negative anchor. Every time you think of learning English you become more nervous and stressed. Most English learners have built up really strong negative anchors, with the passage of time. But you can break and reprogramme these negative anchors following certain steps. They will allow you to change an unwanted negative feeling to a resourceful happy feeling in a few seconds.

Our emotions are things that we can potentially get control of if we approach things in the right way. Imagination and emotions both are a part of our subconscious.

1. Decide how you want to feel

Chances are you very well know how you don't want to feel. You don't want to feel nervous, anxious, or worried. But here you need to think about how you want to feel. It should not be, I want to feel, "Not nervous', 'Not worried', Not anxious. When we think this way, we are focussing on negative emotions. Instead of moving away from them, we are inevitably enhancing them.

So you need to set a positive target. You may want to feel more confident, feel more motivated or maybe you just want to feel calm so that you can focus on thinking clearly. You know how you want to feel, but it should be defined as a positive emotion.

2. Write it in bold

Once you have decided on your positive feelings. You need to grab a sheet of paper and write down that feeling in big bold letters. You need to write it like an affirmation. Make it about you and make sure you write it in the present tense. Make it specific. For example,

I feel confident when I speak in English.

I feel motivated when I speak in English

I can speak English calmly, powerfully, and clearly.

You are training your brain to provide you with a certain feeling. Don't hesitate, even if your request seems to be slightly vague.

3. Create a positive emotional state

Keep looking at that paper and think about the biggest success you have ever had in your life. Think about your future success, speaking English fluently and confidently. Smile to yourself. Let that smile grow bigger. You can feel your entire body filled with positivity. Your body posture will change to a more confident one.

You can use your body even more to give you a better positive feeling. Don't simply stand and smile. Pick up that sheet of paper high in the air. Jump and shout out the words written on the paper loudly as if you are announcing to the world.

Research states, "the deliberate control of motor behavior could regulate feelings." You will notice that every time you repeat the words loudly, they seem to fuel the process. Everything will turn brighter and stronger in your mind. Imagine all the positivity rushing into your body, through every nerve-muscle, and fiber of your being. As it flows through you and fills you up completely take a deep breath and feel all that positivity. Keep repeating the words loudly.

4. Connect

At some point of time, you will feel that everything has turned into reality the way you wanted it to be. This is the peak emotional state. At this very moment, you need to connect this positive peak emotional state with English and start practicing your English lessons- listening to easy English audio. While you are listening keep that cheerful attitude on, keep smiling keep moving around, and let the oxygen flow into your body

This should not be a one-day practice. Every day before you start your English lessons, you need to create a positive emotional state and connect these strong positive feelings with English. In this way gradually you will break all the negative anchors, replacing them with new positive anchors. The more times you do it, the stronger those feelings become and the better you feel. Every time thereafter you listen to or speak English you will feel positive and excited.

It is proven (chapter 5) that when we feel energized and motivated and we enjoy the process without any stress or boredom, our brain can learn faster and retain information longer. The students perform better in positive emotional states. So, all you need is to 'train your brain'. You will speak English fluently and naturally once you connect your brain with your positive emotional state.

CHAPTER TWELVE

How to stay motivated? – Set Strong Goals

All organizations start with WHY, but only the great ones keep their WHY clear year after year. People don't buy what you do; they buy why you do it."

— Simon Sinek, Start with Why: How Great Leaders Inspire Everyone to Take Action

The example he uses most often is computers. When you make up your mind to buy a computer, you will find companies telling you, "We have the computer that works the fastest, it's the most powerful, it's got the newest technology". But when you look at Apple, it has really created a cult following around its brand. They use a completely different style of marketing their products. They started with "WHY". So, where all the other companies were starting with 'what', Apple started with 'why'. Do you remember an old Apple commercial, the tagline says, "Think Different"? They say it clearly, "you must buy an apple product to think differently." The people who own a computer, an iPhone, or any other gadget from Apple, become a part of that counter-culture who think differently.

This proved to be very successful for Apple, as it set them apart from the competition. It allowed them to do things that didn't seem to make a lot of sense for other computer brands. For instance, creating a cell phone.

What is the relevance of this example, to an English learner? The fact is this principle applies not only to the companies but the individuals as well.

Have a powerful WHY

English is no longer just a foreign language in the school curriculum and no longer the sole domain of England. It is the world's second language now. English represents hope for a better future. A future where the world has a common language to solve common problems. And how many people are trying to learn English worldwide, by the way – 2 billion of them. In Latin America, South East Asia, China, and most of all India.

Today English is the language used in the proceedings of the supreme court. The constitution of India declared English, as the Associate official Language. Major government documentation is done in English. English is the primary language in the private, corporate as well as banking sector. A total of 67 countries and 27 non-sovereign entities, use English as an official language, so international business and bilateral deals require English as a communication language. The world's most important institutions like the UNO, NATO & European Union use English as an official language. Most of the technologies used in India are received from English Nations, all the higher and technical education is available in English. More than 50% of the content produced on the internet is in English, the internet usage becomes easy with the knowledge of English. The list goes endless. Is this information enough to motivate you to learn English?

Have you ever thought, "Why do you want to learn English?" Having a powerful "why" to learn English can help you set yourself apart from many people, who have quite superficial reasons for 'Why they are learning English?'

This is so important, that I make all my students do this exercise to discover their own 'WHY' for learning English. The question that might be flustering your mind would be,

"What is the reason to do it?" or "how's it going to help me?"

It's quite possible when you think of learning English, you think of it as something that you 'have to do.' Let's consider a few things that you've had to do in your past. For example, maybe when you were young, your parents would ask you to do the chores, make up the bed, and throw the trash. Or maybe they tell you that you have to do your homework. Your teachers may tell you; that you have to study for the test. Probably those were the things you had to do, not what you really wanted to do. You probably didn't care about them much. You weren't passionate about them.

Shifting your attitude allows you to shift your motivation to a completely different level. This is the reason it is so important to discover your "WHY." This is something that will propel you forward, it will light a fire inside you, and it will make you passionate about learning English. So, your mindset will shift from, "I have to learn English" to "I want to learn English", to "I love learning English." This feeling is very significant.

Every individual's WHY is going to be unique to them. And there can be different levels of WHY ranging from deeper to more superficial. Let's say you are reading this book, you might 'have to learn English or you 'Want to learn English' because you need English for professional purposes. That's great! If you want to be successful, it's very important to know English, so that you get a promotion or an appraisal or you may start your entrepreneurship journey. But there can be much wider and deeper 'WHYs' of learning English. The next level of finding your 'WHY' can be thinking about needing your English because you want to travel or because you want to pursue higher studies (most of the higher studies are available in English) or maybe you want to make friends from other countries.

But if we take it a level deeper, you may understand the kind of impact English fluency can have on human consciousness, global interconnectivity, and the way that we perceive ourselves as a part of the world. Wherever you are in the spectrum of motivation to learn English is completely fine. What's important is that it should change as you progress in your English learning journey.

The exercise

1. Grab a paper and a pen
2. Write down, "Why am I learning English?"

Write whatever comes to your mind in the very first instance. So your first answer may be a bit superficial, a bit simpler, something that has been induced into your brain by the education system or society. These goals are weak and uninspiring. They feel more like an obligation. Weak goals produce weak results.

For example. You may write, "I am learning English because I want to get a better job." "Travel internationally". "Score good marks in IELTS or TOEFL exams."

1. Now, ask yourself "WHY?" five times.

Let's say, you write, "I am learning English to score good marks on the IELTS exam."

1. Why do you want to score good marks in the IELTS exam?

   Because I want better job opportunities.

2. Why do you want better job opportunities?

   Because I want to earn more money.

3. Why do you want to earn more money?

I want to earn more money for my family.

4. Why do you want to earn more money for your family?

   I love them and I want to provide them with a better life.

5. Why do you want to give them a better life?

   Because I want them to have more opportunities than I had.

So, this is your big real strong goal. This strong goal will motivate you to learn English intensely, it will create positive and powerful emotions in your mind. This will direct all your actions towards success. You will never be able to get it out of your mind. It will moreover become a positive addiction for you. It will act as a north star, even in difficult times. It will energize you, and inspire you to an extent that you will never give up. Your big real gaol acts as fuel to your burning desire to learn English.

4. Prepare a 'GOAL CARD'

Write down this powerful inspiring goal on any old visiting card, on the blank side, and put it in your wallet. Not just keep it there, review it several times a day. The reason why you are doing this is that when you constantly keep coming in contact with it, it is going to help you to continue that motivation to always feel inspired by it and you come back to the deeper purpose of learning English.

Another way of doing this is you can take a picture of this card and set it as a screensaver on your phone. So, every time you look at your phone you are reminded of your big 'WHY' for learning English, your real goal, and that will turn out to be a huge motivation for you.

Ignite your passion

Choose big, strong, challenging, powerful goals. These goals must give you the power and energy to ACT. The goals should make you want to jump out of bed every morning. They just want you to learn more and become a better version of yourself with each passing day. Why do you want to learn English? What inspires you to learn English? What will you achieve after becoming fluent in English? Think huge, dream larger.

Meditate to speak fluent English

If you want to speak fluently, confidently and with a calm mind, your emotional stability is a must. You should be emotionally calm composed and stable. You should be able to handle the nervousness and fear, whenever you come across fluent English speakers or you need to speak in front of a group of people or make a stage presentation. The ability to handle your emotions and thoughts defines your emotional stability. Meditation plays a vital role in achieving that.

Meditation helps you to become a confident English speaker, and a better communicator, it helps you to handle your negative emotions like fear, nervousness, stress, and anxiety, when you speak with fluent English speakers or stand on stage.

Communication is all about your psychology, it has a close relationship with your mindset, beliefs, attitude, and emotions. But we are ingrained to think that communication is all about speaking grammatically correct English using impressive vocabulary words and phrases. Many times, you get nervous while speaking, you may even forget the words or sentences out of anxiety. You may even end up saying something which was not a part of the preparation or planning.

It is very important to handle your emotions and make your mind stable. If your mind is disturbed, there will be no effective communication. Effective communication happens when you are able to understand the other person and answer in a way that the listener interprets the message correctly. Communication is a result of a stable mind. To put it precisely, the words which flow out of your mouth are the mirror image of what is happening inside your mind.

Research has shown, that meditation has been linked to increased ability to focus and to lower depression, anxiety, and stress. Meditation is an act of focusing one's thoughts completely and fully. It is being present in the moment, silencing other thoughts and noise running through our minds. Neuroscience has shown that the brain can absorb information and retain memory when in a relaxed state. Meditation can help one achieve such a state, thereby improving a student's memory and attention (Machado 2014).

Communication is all about making mistakes. When you make a mistake people will laugh at you, they will judge you, and make fun of you. To deal with all this meditation and peace of mind are important.

In my course I make students do meditation every day for 10 minutes. I have seen the people who are not willing to meditate are the people who lose their calm very easily, they get nervous while speaking, they make more mistakes, and they get hurt easily when corrected or made fun of by other people.

Meditate daily for at least 10 minutes to achieve a stable calm and composed mind which can lower your nervousness and fear of English, in other words, lower your affective filters and help you not only acquire English better and faster but also help you speak English fluently and confidently.

CHAPTER THIRTEEN

PLAYING IT BY THE EARS

There are four language parts or four parts to any language learning. Two understanding ones or the inputs- reading and listening. Two are the expressional ones or the output- writing and speaking. An individual has experiences that get converted into thoughts and ideas, which are conveyed to others in form of a message. This can be done in two ways writing or speaking. Listening is the term used for the ability to understand spoken language and reading are used for understanding the written language. In day-to-day life an individual is engaged in various communication activities, involving written and spoken conversations. Spoken conversations involve both talking and listening. Listening other than conversations involves listening to oral conferences, oral readings, memorizations, entertainment such as audio and videos, formal talks, directions, and many more.

An article," The importance of listening ability", by Paul T. Rankin, reports that, "The average percentage of waking time devoted to each form of communication was computed for a total of sixty days as recorded by twenty-one different people. In these records, the time listed as the conversation was divided into two, and half recorded as talking and half as listening, on the assumption that, in general, one listens about half the time and talks about half the time during a conversation. For this group of records, nearly *70 percent of the total waking time was spent in some form of communication,* listening ranking first, talking second, reading third, and writing fourth. Oral language stands out very conspicuously as being the most used form of language.

Listening leads to 42.1 percent of the total time spent in communication. The importance of oral language is evident again, both in expression and reception. Talking is used three times as much as the writing; listening is almost three times as much as reading. It is apparent also that the receiving forms, listening and reading, occur much more frequently than the expressional forms, talking and writing. This is to be expected because one person may talk and a hundred listen, or one may write and a thousand people read."

What is fluency?

Fluency is the ability to communicate and understand natural English as it is spoken by the English speakers for which you need to – (1) listen and understand easily and (2) you need to speak smoothly.

"In the medical college, I wasn't able to understand the lectures in English. As I was a student at Hindi medium school, I never asked any questions in the class because I didn't know how to ask questions in English, further, I was afraid, I may speak something wrong or something absolutely out of the context, which may make me a piece of mockery. When I shared my plight with one of my professors, he suggested reading English Newspapers and English books. For a long time, I did that, but there was no improvement. I wasn't able to put my thoughts into words. I was so frustrated. I decided to give up, thinking English is not my cup of tea, until I met you", says Dr. Anugya, one of my students.

Most of the conventional English classes focus on speaking and just speaking from day 1. Input is essential to get the output. You learn more grammar, you understand more words and phrases. No input, no output. You need to listen to more and more English to be able to understand the fluent English speakers or the native speakers. How can you expect to answer a person if you don't understand what he is saying? Comprehending the message is vital for fluent and effective English communication. For this, you need to improve your listening skills.

Analytical English Learning

If you have been following the traditional methods for English learning, it's quite possible, that you learned mostly with your eyes. Most of the teachers, schools, colleges, and universities, focus on textbooks for English learning. They are moreover concentrating on the grammar-translation method, grammar drills, and communication approach.

If this is the way you have been learning English for years, you have been learning English Analytically. Analytical thinkers deal with situations by consciously evaluating the information they've gathered and organized. When you think analytically you tend to solve a problem and find an answer. These analytical thinkers do not rush to conclusions, and question every detail of a problem. English speaking is not a subject where you get problems to solve or you need to find a solution or an answer. English conversations require a quick subconscious response.

Analytical learning is dependent mainly on textbooks, it requires giving sufficient attention in all English language learning contexts. The textbooks are the main sources of input for the learners. This includes Language-form-focused exercises that are traditional ones, like changing the tense of the verb in sentences, making interrogative and negative sentences, filling in the gaps in sentences with certain words, etc. These language-form-focused learning activities, change the nature of learners into consciousness-raising ones as students are made to pay attention to such forms to become fully aware of them. You happen to learn and know a lot about grammar. It is quite possible, that you know more grammar than any native speaker because they don't learn English that way. You learn to think about English, you don't think in English, you can talk about English, you don't talk in English and hence you translate English. You learn how to learn English.

Analytical English vs Real English

Real English	**Analytical English**
Narrative-like	Expository-like
Action-oriented	Idea-oriented
Event-oriented	Argument-oriented
Story-oriented	Explanatory
Here and now	Future and past
Informal	Formal
Natural communication	Artificial communication
Spontaneous	Planned
Ellipsis (omission of understood words)	The explicitness of a textbook consciousness
Structureless	Highly structured
Repetitive	Concise
Simple linear structures	Complex hierarchical structures
Paratactic patterns	Hypotactic patterns
Unconscious	Conscious and structured

The native speakers can speak English naturally and subconsciously. The number one reason for it is that they learn English with their ears, without any formal study of the language. They hear English from their parents, caretakers, neighbors, teachers, and others around them. You can speak your native language fluently because you have learned it similarly.

1. Vocabulary is different

Many of the learners can write good English but they can't speak well. Real English conversations are different than reading. The vocabulary used in everyday English is simpler and more casual in comparison to the vocabulary used in textbooks.

There is a wide range of slang, phrasal verbs, phrases, and idioms used by native speakers. Such students may have learned English in school through textbooks, they may be good readers but may face a lot of difficulty in understanding normal speech.

2. Grammar is different

In real life English, the interlocutors usually do not pay much attention to lexical content and meaning, which are strictly taken care of by the learners who apply the textbook English. In real-life conversations, native speakers usually use incomplete sentences. Consider the following example: People can say, "Just going to check the reserve stock out of the back. Won't be a minute". Whereas a student of English may say, "I am just going to check the reserve stock out the back. It won't be a minute."

Fluent English speakers do not apply strict rules, so they are less rigid and more flexible with grammar. Moreover, people communicate with each other anytime and anywhere, so most of the frequency of English used is informal and less academic. This is the reason why speakers can have chances to use vocatives, expletives, exclamations, and abbreviations.

3. Speed is fast

The native speakers speak fast, sometimes they even tend to swallow sounds. For example, when saying, 'Last summer I joined the basketball practices." The sound of "D" in the word joined may not be audible clearly, but it's still there. Similarly, when saying, "I need some water to quench my thirst." The word water may sound like, “wattuh” with no distinct sound of “R”.

We are talking about the English that you are using in your daily life. We are not talking about the English you are using in the classrooms, or when you are passing an interview at Harvard. Native speakers do not speak academic English. Many times, it is difficult to understand the fast English spoken by natives or fluent speakers. There are many reasons for it. You have no time to think about translations or grammar rules or the textbook lessons or the pronunciations. Your brain tries to catch up with the words and it becomes quite overwhelming and unclear. This is the reason you find it difficult to understand a conversation between two native speakers. Understanding English movies, web series, and shows becomes challenging for you. Your conscious brain cannot analyze, translate and organize at the same time. As a result, your speech becomes really slow.

Listening is the foundation of speaking

Research proves that speech happens as a result of listening. A child’s sense of hearing starts to develop at a really early stage in life. Research has shown that babies develop the power to listen within the womb and can respond within days of birth to their mother’s voice. Babies start listening and reacting to noises, sounds, and voices at a really young age. By the time they’re four months old, a baby will turn towards the sound of a voice. As a child grows, they learn to listen to different sounds, discriminate between them, and recognize voices and sounds from the world around them. Eventually, children will develop the ability to find, differentiate between and identify sounds, and understand them (in words and sentences). They listen to the language for a long time before he begins to speak. This period is called the ‘*silent period*’. This period is absolutely crucial for the development of speech, phonological awareness, and ultimately, reading. Listening is a crucial skill for young children to acquire. Listening is one of the basic building blocks of language and communication.

Listening-a Macro Skill in language learning

Listening has a significant role to play in learning as it is one of the four major skills in language acquisition. Although other skills such as reading, speaking, and writing are vital to developing language competency, listening contributes primarily to language expertise. Listening brings awareness of the language as it is a receptive skill that first develops in a human being. Learning to listen to a language improves language ability. The sound, rhythm, intonation, and stress of the language can only be perfectly acquired through listening. To understand the nuances in English, one must be willing and able to listen to English. As we get to understand spoken English by listening it is easier to improve our other skills and gain confidence. Listening helps English learners to understand the beauty of the language. It provides the aural input and enables learners to interact in spoken communication Thus listening forms the firm basis for complete English proficiency. Other than being the primary form of communication, it forms the basis of English language teaching too.

Listening ability will always be higher than speaking ability

Your speaking ability grows with your listening ability. Imagine sowing a seed in the ground. You will need to nurture this seed by watering it now and then. Only then the seed will grow into a healthy plant. Similarly, the potential for speaking English (the seed, the template – chapter 5) is already there in your brain. All you need to do is to nurture it with a lot of understandable listening (comprehensible input- chapter 5).

Consider children, they are always able to understand more English than they could speak. The reason is they start listening much earlier. Your listening ability will always be higher than your speaking ability. Some students complain," I can understand

English more than I can speak." You need to understand that this is a natural process.

Imagine your listening ability as a hot air balloon and your speaking ability as the compartment tied to it. The higher your listening ability goes, the better will be your speaking ability. The balloon pulls the compartment along but it will always be higher than it.

Why don't we listen sometimes?

Listening is the most neglected skill. People often only hear what is being said. Although the hearing is a lot different from listening. Listening requires making a conscious effort not to just hear what people are saying but to take it in, digest it and understand. Not only does listening enhance your comprehension ability and make you an effective communicator, but it also makes you an interesting speaker. The people will enjoy listening to you. But, why don't we listen sometimes? Our habits or our circumstances and environment may often affect our listening. It is quite easy to become distracted by something, or by our own thoughts which disengage us from what is being said. Some of the reasons why we don't properly listen are:

- Being occupied in our thoughts
- Being distracted by something
- We may be busy framing a response
- Something conflicting with our opinion

Listening makes English less stressful

In most conventional English classes, the students are pushed to speak right from the very initial stages, this is an unnatural approach. In fact, this can have the opposite effect on your English learning making it slow and stressful. The reason is, that your brain is not acquainted with a few new words. On the other hand, it is not able to process the new words and store them in your memory.

So, you will not be able to understand what an English speaker is speaking. This will lead to frustration and stress.

One major advantage of spending your maximum time on listening activities is, that it helps reduce the stress and anxiety you may feel while speaking English. In a study of beginning-level English students, it was found that the learners who weren't forced to speak but were trained in listening comprehension, performed better than the students trained using traditional methods.

This may not be necessary for intermediate learners, although you may try. For beginners, it works like magic. Your speaking will improve subconsciously.

80% of English learning time should involve listening

Listening is the most significant part of English learning. It is pivotal in providing a substantial and meaningful response. It helps the learner to acquire pronunciation, word stress, vocabulary, and syntax and the comprehension of messages conveyed can be based solely on tone of voice, pitch, and accent; and it is only possible when we listen. Without understanding input appropriately, learning simply cannot get any improvement. In addition, without listening skills, no communication can be achieved.

'Also, every study conducted regarding the language skills acquisition has proved that when we communicate, we gain 45% of language competence from listening, 30% from speaking, 15% from reading, and 10% from writing.'

Listening has all its interrelated subskills such as receiving, understanding, remembering, evaluating, and responding. This is the reason, 80% of your English learning time should involve listening activities.

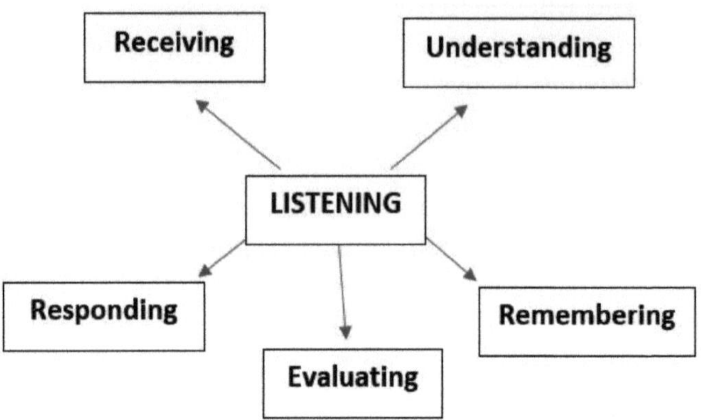
Receiving
Understanding
LISTENING
Responding
Remembering
Evaluating

CHAPTER FOURTEEN

LEARN WITH YOUR EARS

We understand that listening is the most important of the four skills of language learning. An individual spends, 42.1 percent of the total time spent in communication, on listening. And, we gain 45% of language competence from listening.

The question is, how to do that? What is the best way to do that? How many hours should I spend listening to English and how can I spend contact hours on English in meaningful ways?

For many of us, English is not our native language. We don't have many opportunities to speak with English speakers and maybe many of us don't also have the confidence to do so. So, how can you turn your attention, your focus from grammar and vocabulary and translation towards more speaking and listening?

If you want to get better at something you need to focus on it, you need to do it consistently. Suppose, you need to reduce weight. Then you need to keep a continuous check on your weight, you need to keep a check on your diet, and you need to follow the exercises which can help you reduce your weight. If you want to be a better speaker and better listener you need to do listening and speaking exercises and need to do them relentlessly. When you listen to English you speak better English and you read English you write good English.

What to listen to? - The 3Es

1. EASY- Listen to something easy

I remember when I was in school, whenever my mother attended the parent's meeting, the teacher told her to make me watch the English news and read the English newspaper. The very next day I was made to sit in front of the television watching BBC News. Did that help? Did I even understand anything? Was I able to use that English in my real life?

As English learners, we find it dignified to say, "I am watching the CNN news", rather than saying, "I am watching a kid's show".

If you listen to something very difficult, you might feel frustrated if you don't understand the meaning of what you are listening to. You might give up. Nobody wants to listen to very difficult stuff making it very difficult for us to understand. So, I would suggest listening to something easy. By easy I mean you should be able to understand at least 85 to 90% of the content.

Remember Dr. Stephen Krashen's idea of Comprehensible Input. (Chapter 5). *"The best methods are therefore those that supply 'comprehensible input' in low anxiety situations, containing messages that students really want to hear. These methods do not force early production in the second language, but allow students to produce when they are 'ready', recognizing that improvement comes from supplying communicative and comprehensible input, and not from forcing and correcting production."*

Suppose, if you are able to grasp only 50% of what you are listening to, it is of no use. No understanding, no learning. No learning, no improvement. Gradually, you will be ready for more difficult and advanced, but to start with listening to a lot of easy English material

I would suggest you go for some news or maybe some serials or some series, which you have already watched in your native language. That makes it easier to understand what is happening and then you can relate to the words the speakers are speaking in English. In the case of some sports commentary also you at least have an understanding of what is happening. You can choose kids' programs, and kids' audiobooks. You can listen to audio of articles or speeches; you may use text to refer to while listening. Advanced learners may use movies along with subtitles, So, go for something easy

2. ENJOYABLE- Listen to something interesting

Whatever you are listening to, should be interesting and relaxing for you. For instance, if you have no interest in cricket, and you go for listening to a cricket podcast, it will not interest you. You will not be bothered to listen to it. Listen to something, which is interesting for you, which is enjoyable for you, which you are willing to listen to, and not only listen to which you are willing to discuss with others. It should provoke your thoughts and imagination. This kind of listening will stimulate your brain and keep you interested in what you are listening to. Nobody wants to listen to the boring stuff. You can go for a political podcast. You can go for a football podcast or maybe if you are interested in listening to motivational audios or videos

3. ENDLESSLY - Listen a lot

A lot means a lot. Just listening to something, a bit here and a bit there would not help it will not help you to improve quickly. The more English you put in, the more you'll get out!

The best English listening activities

Now you are clear, with what to listen to. The next step is to choose your activities. The following are the best English listening exercises and activities that I recommend to all of my students.

1. Podcast

A podcast is an audio show. They are recordings of English conversations or speeches, which you can download from the internet for free. This is the practice that I still do and what I started with. The very best way to improve your listening skills is through podcasts. This is my opinion as a professional English Trainer and a language learner.

The research was conducted on, 'The Impact of Podcasts on EFL Students' Listening Comprehension'. It was published in the *International Journal of Language Education. Faculty of Languages and Literature UNM Jl Daeng Tata Raya Makassar, South Sulawesi.* Findings revealed that Podcast has a significant impact on students' listening comprehension. Additionally, the students have a positive attitude toward the use of podcasts in the listening classroom. Students perceived that podcasts provided authentic materials, interesting activities including listening exercises, and meaningful tasks for them so they felt more motivated to learn English.

How to use podcasts to improve English listening?

These are the most effective steps to using podcasts to learn English.

Find a good English podcast at your level.

One is, of course, The Fearless Communicators Tribe, my talk show (https://anchor.fm/jain-surabhi) but there are hundreds available on various platforms. Choose something easy and interesting.

Listen first without a transcript or subtitles.

Try to first listen to the podcast without any help. It may be possible that the podcast you are listening to comes with a transcript or key vocabulary, don't look at it the first time you listen to it. This will force you to really understand the context of what has been said.

You can keep noting down the words that you don't understand as you go along. Sometimes you will realize what they mean there and then, just by writing them down. Sometimes, you write down a word, then later on in the podcast, you realize what it means, as it is used again in a different context. Doing this means that you have **actively** discovered the meaning and you're more likely to remember the word or expression. Additionally, it's much more interesting to learn vocabulary and grammar **in context**, which means to hear or read them as part of a normal sentence and understand the meaning, than to learn them from a textbook.

Use a transcript or subtitles.

These aids will help you figure out anything you missed on the first listen and also reinforce new vocab or phrases. Speech can be followed with the help of the transcript. Check the transcript before looking at the key vocabulary, for any word that you can't understand. At times, the pronunciation can be different from your expectation. Make sure you listen to the entire podcast without the transcript at least one time before opening it. Just reading the transcript as you listen along will make it easier to understand, but push yourself to try to understand it without the transcript first. If you are listening to a podcast that has a vocabulary list with it, use that only if you can't understand a word in the transcript.

Change the speed of the podcast

One of the major complaints from the English learners is that the speed of the English speaker is too fast to understand. This isn't a problem with podcasts. If you feel it's too fast? You can slow the speed down. If you feel it's too easy and you want to push yourself? Speed it up. You will actually be surprised at how well you can understand.

Write a summary.

This is one way to make sure that you're learning English actively and will also help in developing your writing skills. Write a summary of what the podcast was about. What were the key points? What were your takeaways? Did you agree or disagree with everything that was said?

It helps to improve your comprehension skills. If you can summarise everything that has been said, accurately, this means that you have understood the main idea of the podcast. If you didn't understand every word, this is fine, as long as you have understood the main things and the context. Moreover, it gives you a chance to put new pieces of vocabulary, sentence structures, or expressions that you heard used in the podcast, into use. The new vocabulary can be memorized, recalled, and used only through practicing them yourself and contextualizing them.

2. YouTube videos

YouTube videos are another interesting way to keep your phone full of English content. The best part about YouTube videos is you can subscribe to the channels of your interest and to add on it keeps suggesting videos as per your liking. One thing you can do in YouTube videos is you can reduce the speed. It will help you to listen more clearly and understand accent and pronunciation better. You can subscribe to my YouTube channel at https://youtube.com/c/SURABHIJAIN.

How to use YouTube to learn English?

Choose good videos.

They should be *comprehensible* to you at your level, you should be able to understand 85- 90% of the context, they should be *interesting*to you, and they should be *short* (so that you can watch them multiple times).

Just watch.

First, watch in English with English subtitles. Take care, as the subtitles are automatically generated by YouTube, they often have mistakes in them.

Watch a second time.

This time, watch with subtitles in your native language only if you struggled to understand the English subtitles. This will help you understand what is happening in the video.

Watch a third time.

Watch again. This time with English subtitles. By now, you should have a good understanding of the meaning of the video so you are likely to grab more words or speech.

Watch a fourth time.

This time, take notes of words and phrases you don't know and find out their meanings.

Take a deep breath, and watch a fifth time.

This time, watch without subtitles. Now you understand the content and new words better and you should be able to understand most of the video.

3. Audiobooks

This is again a wonderful way of listening to English. The audiobook is a recording of a book or other work being read out loud. Many paid and free apps on which you can find audiobooks are available. For example, audiobooks from Audibles from Amazon is a paid app and the Audiobook app is a free app.

Passive Listening

Passive listening is where you are receiving content, and your brain is just absorbing, letting the information flow over you. It is turning off your conscious brain and letting the subconscious mind do its job. This involves listening to a lot of understandable and interesting English speech and doing it repetitively. As you listen your brain tries to understand the meaning of the whole context. You silence your conscious brain. You don't need to worry about the words you don't understand. Your mind is open and quiet. You are relaxed and just let English wash over you.

A few examples of **passive listening** would be:

- Watching a film on Netflix / YouTube
- Listening to a podcast while gardening or cooking
- Listening to a YouTube video while waiting at the doctor's or traveling on public transport.
- Joining an 'English conversation group' on Messenger or WhatsApp
- Just 'being' in an English-speaking country without really engaging with people

Active listening

Active listening is different from passive listening. Your brain is wired to passive listening only. We need to make a conscious effort to do active listening. It takes practice and time to master. Active listening is fully concentrating on what is being said, understanding and accepting it without pre-judgment rather than hearing the general message.

Active learning means that you are conscious of your language learning, rather than expecting that your English will just improve through absorption, and actively forcing your brain to get into gear.

You need to flex your language learning muscles, you need to make them do the work that will help you retain the new words, phrases, and grammar structures that you come across.

Examples of **active listening** include:

- Listening to podcasts in English (*and following the steps I have mentioned above*)
- Listening to native speakers in conversations (*and listening very carefully to exactly how they use certain expressions*)
- Creating your own vocabulary flashcards and vocabulary books (*not just using readymade stuff*)
- Reading in English (*and actively looking up for the meaning of the words and phrases you don't know*)
- Writing in English (this doesn't include, *chatting on WhatsApp or Facebook groups*)
- Speaking in English (*and trying to use all of your new expressions*)

Both passive and active listening are equally significant for mastering English.

Studies suggest that around 60% of learners are 'passive' learners, only 10% are 'active' learners, and the remaining 30% are 'blocked'. Passive learning activities can be more fun. For instance, putting on a film in English at the end of a tiring day, from an English learning point of view, is much better than putting on a film in your native language. One of the main advantages of passive listening is that you can listen to English *while doing something else*. Whether that's driving, riding on the bus or metro, out running, or at home doing chores, podcasts in English allow you to learn (passively) while doing something that you would be doing anyway. That is a complete win-win situation.

The reason you have picked up this book is that you are really serious about improving your English. You may have a particular goal in mind. If you want to become a fluent, fearless, natural, and confident speaker, then you need to find a balance between passive listening and active listening activities.

7-dayExercise – Practice with Netflix or Movies

Hollywood movies are a great way to learn English. These days people enjoy binge-watching. You can also use Netflix as an effective source for English learning. But just watching them passively will not help you improve. Sometimes it might be frustrating or boring if you don't understand what is happening in the movie or series due to language constraints. To overcome this problem, you need to follow a proper trajectory and use these sources wisely for active learning.

- **Choose a show.** Again, choose something easy and interesting which you like and also something relatively short so you can re-watch it easily. A 20-minute episode is ideal.
- **Enjoy watching the first day.** Watch the whole episode in English with English subtitles. Do not use subtitles in your language. It's fine if you don't understand everything. If you really struggled to understand the English, rewatch this scene with subtitles in your language.
- **Second day.** Pick up your favorite scene & watch it again several times. Focus on this scene with complete attention. It should be about 2 to 5 minutes. At any point, if you don't understand, you may pause and take notes on new words or phrases that you come across. Lookup for the meanings of the words and phrases in the dictionary or on google. Keep rewatching the scene until you understand all the words completely.

- **Third & Fourth day.** This time, watch the scene with English subtitles multiple times. Keep reviewing your list of words and phrases wherever required. Turn off the subtitles. Then watch it again. You will find that you have a better sense of what they're saying. You will be able to listen closely to the language they are using. Repeating the same scene again and again for many days might seem overwhelming, but with each repetition, you are improving your listening ability for English.
- **Fifth day.** Watch the scene again, but this time, use *Imitation Technique*

The imitation method is one of the fastest ways of improving spoken English.

How to use IMITATION TECHNIQUE?

1. Find a video or audio recorded by an English speaker.
2. Now play the video or audio and
3. As you listen try to imitate the speaker sentence by sentence. When the speaker has spoken a sentence pause the audio and try to repeat the entire sentence word by word.

If you think that this exercise is super simple and easy, let me tell you it's not. Why? because English speakers often use long and complex sentences. So how to imitate sentences like this? The key is- *to memorize a few words at a time.* don't wait until the speaker completes the entire sentence because then you will not be able to remember anything. What to do? After a few words have been spoken pause the video and repeat the words immediately. Whenever you are imitating a native speaker, you should imitate a few words at a time.

If you are thinking, oh forget it, it doesn't work in this way. You are imitating a speaker and you will be able to speak fluently.

Let me tell you I have been trying this technique to improve my spoken English for a long time and I have been teaching this technique to my students for years, with excellent results. Some people think this practice is not at all effective because all you are doing is repeating the English speakers mindlessly like a parrot. There is no thinking involved.

This technique has great results with any second language learning. A study reports interviews with three university English majors who had won prizes in nationwide English-speaking competitions and debate tournaments in China. The imitation practice enabled them to attend to and learn collocations and sequences, borrow these sequences for productive use, to improve pronunciation, and to develop the habit of attending to details of language in the context of language input. The paper concludes that such practice enhances noticing and rehearsal and hence facilitates second language acquisition.

The practice is not as easy as it seems it requires you to imitate and recall long and complex sentences from your memory. It can be quite challenging, especially for beginners.

- **Sixth day.** Practice the scene several times with imitation again.
- **Seventh-day.** Relax, and watch the entire episode again. Finally, watch the whole episode again. You still might face problems in understanding everything in the whole episode, but by now you will have "mastered" a piece of it. Once you go through the entire movie or series in this way, you should see lots of improvement in your English listening.

Passive speaking

This is your ultimate goal. When you speak English passively, you just let the words flow out. You don't worry about mistakes. You don't think about rules. You don't analyze your speech or struggle to fit in words. You don't focus on translations. The words pour out of your mouth SUBCONSCIOUSLY, automatically, and naturally. For this kind of level of speaking, we need to practice both passive and active listening. The ultimate goal of all the active listening lessons inside the **Turbo English Mastery** Program is to enable you to speak naturally and subconsciously.

CHAPTER FIFTEEN

PHRASEOLOGY- POWER OF PHRASES

We understand that learning grammar is not an efficient way to learn a new language. Memorizing text is not efficient. Vocabulary is the most important of all to be able to communicate in any language. But, just reading and memorizing lists of "individual words" is not worthful. Looking words up in a dictionary is not efficient. What is efficient?

But before that let us understand, *why not learn individual words.*

1. Cramming

Remember in schools we had those long lists of new and difficult words and then we found out their meanings in the dictionary. Then we crammed those words along with their meanings, probably we fetched good scores for that. But how many of you remember those crammed words or how many of you use those words in your daily speaking? For sure the textbook method didn't work.

2. Memorizing conjugations

Suppose the word you encounter is a verb you also start memorizing the conjugations. For example, He runs, she runs, they run, Arun runs, I run, and so on. Lots of memorization indeed.

3. Translation

Many English learners have a habit of noting down the translation of the new vocabulary word in their native language, along with the word. This makes the situation even worse. When speaking in English you first think of the word in your own language, then translate it into English. This causes extra work inside your brain making your speech slow and broken.

What is efficient? - Phrases

Learning phrases and learning them in their natural context is efficient. Phrases are groups of words that naturally belong together. A phrase is a group of words put together in order. Sometimes it may have a meaning different from the meaning of all individual words put together. Therefore, you have to memorize and remember the entire phrase.

What does that mean? It means that while a phrase is made up of multiple words (all of which have their own function), all of the words work together to perform one larger function. They kind of remind me of a choir. A choir is made up of individual voices, but all of the voices come together to sing one song.

Typically, these phrases are 2-5 words long. The same phrases are put into use over and again. These phrases are formed by how the native speakers put words together. Some words belong together in certain situations and a few don't. You've got to mix the words. You've got to learn them in a certain way so that the meaning is obvious. A native speaker knows how certain words group together naturally. A learner doesn't have this sense and requires to develop it.

Power of phrases

When you learn to talk in a new language whether English or any other second language, you ought to pay attention to the phrases that are utilized in that language. you need to specialize in English phrases, not individual words. Once you save a new word, try saving the phrase along with it sometimes. It'll assist you to remember how the word is used and what it means. It boosts your learning. Learn phrases to learn English naturally!

Phrases are one of the foremost important factors that decide whether or not you'll be able to speak a foreign language well enough in a short period. What makes phrases so important to your success?

1. Context

It is once you get the phrases right that your English is going to be fluent, not once you have learned all the concepts of grammar. In Turbo English Mastery, we place great emphasis on learning phrases. We've created a system that accelerates the training of phrases in their natural context.

Each situation where you require English is exclusive and unpredictable. Most sentences you'll use are going to be unique and can depend upon the requirements of a specific situation.

Imagine you would like to move into a hotel or visit the post office. You can't expect things you face there to match the dialogue in your textbook. And there are numerous possible situations, more than the post office and the railway station and the hospital and other scenarios that you simply find in textbooks.

You need flexible tools. Yes, you have to learn words, many words, words for each situation. Listening to more & more English helps you to find out words, efficiently and in context. But that's not enough. You furthermore may get to find out how these words group together to form sense in English. That's why you must learn phrases. These phrases are based on how the native speakers put words together. Some words belong together in certain situations and some do not. You have to combine the words you have learned in a certain way so that the meaning is clear.

2. Understanding the spoken English

Learning English phrases makes it so much easier to understand what you hear. Phrases are used in virtually any conversation of native English speakers. If you want to improve your English listening quickly, you must learn the way native speakers speak, learn the phrases they often use.

3. Easy to memorize & recall

It is easier to memorize and recall a long-phrase or sentence than a single word. This fact is specifically a truth when forming listening skills because you will be able to recognize more and understand better, a long-phrase than a single word. These are phrases that are used most of the time. So, just focus, and listen carefully, you'll hear them used a lot.

When you grab more English phrases, understanding spoken English will be easy as pie (very easy) for you. For instance, "His name is on the tip of my tongue, wait a minute."

4. Reading faster

Phrases group are several words together in a written text. When you start looking at phrases as a single unit, with a specific meaning, you'll be a faster English reader. Instead of spending time thinking about what each individual English word means, you will be able to group a few words together in phrases as you read.

Since you'll spot and understand what the phrases mean, you'll save time reading through a text—but you'll understand its meaning even better if you just knew what each word meant. For example, "*I was wondering if* the manager would agree with my design."

5. Improving your Grammar

If you have trouble with prepositions, the use of the article, or verb tenses, then you should save phrases that can help you get a feel for how to overcome these problems. If you regularly revisit your phrases you will begin to notice them in everything you read and listen to. You will understand English better. Soon you would be capable of using these phrases in your writing and speaking. You will make fewer mistakes with prepositions, articles, and verb tenses. Soon you will be able to use vocabulary more naturally.

For example, "I would spend my weekend *on an island.*" When we learn this as a phrase, we automatically acquire the preposition "*on*an island" as well as the article, "*an* island". When you use this in your speaking you won't have to think about these two separately and it will cut the unnecessary steps involved, making your speech fluent and confident.

Another example is with verbs. Suppose instead of learning the word 'Abhor' individually, you learn, "He abhors cats." You are learning the most crucial part of grammar where most of the learners commit a mistake- 'the subject-verb agreement, but you are learning it subconsciously. You learn grammar from just that word in the phrase, that's on the end, abhors. In the future whenever you will say "He abhors cats.", you will add the 's' because that is how you learned it. There will be no delay in speaking because you don't need to think about conjugations of the verb 'abhor'. You have learned it correctly from a phrase and now it's used subconsciously.

6. Improving your spoken English

The same thing happens when you speak. If you use phrases when you speak, native speakers will be more likely to understand what you want to say although your pronunciation may not be really good yet.

Let's say you question a native English speaker: "Is your health good?" as a greeting, he may not understand. As far as grammar structure is concerned, this sentence is correct. But native English speakers still do not get it, the reason being, that they never say it that way. In other words, the sound, in this case, is not familiar to them in this particular context. However, if you say: "how are you?" or "how are you doing?", they will understand instantly no matter how poor your pronunciation is. Learning the phrases that native English speakers commonly use is one of the quickest ways to learn Spoken English.

A better understanding of the listener gives you a kind of acceptance that results in confidence and creates an upward spiral of empowering beliefs. (Chapter 10)

7. Improves your pronunciation

Many English learners speak with strange rhythm and intonation. Rhythm and intonation are the music of a language. Every language has a music. When you worry about the pronunciation of individual sounds and words, your pronunciation becomes robotic.

The native speakers and fluent English speakers speak in phrases, taking pauses naturally between phrases. These natural pauses create a rhythm of English. The pronunciation is clear and comprehensible because they have learned English through phrases.

Many English learners learn English through word-by-word translation, by memorizing every word individually. This is the reason they tend to speak English word by word, one at a time. As a result, they take pauses at unnatural places, creating strange word groupings. This follows a broken and artificial rhythm that is very difficult to be understood by the natives. This becomes quite frustrating for the listener and embarrassing for the speaker.

So, learn English through phrases and speak with a natural rhythm and intonation.

Where to find phrases?

The next important question is, where to get these phrases? And what are the phrases worth learning. One easy way to find useful phrases is in my **Power Booster Phrases** course where I share a 30-day challenge to help you learn everyday English phrases. It is a systematic course, which will help you to understand the natives clearly. Along with that, you can speak fluently and effortlessly using those phrases in your daily life.

Apart from this, you can find abundant phrases in any natural English content you watch, listen or read. Be focussed on such phrases and keep writing them down.

How to record a phrase?

I recommend you maintain a phrase bank. Whenever you read or hear a new word or phrase, write it in your notebook. The minute you discover new English vocabulary in a lesson, in a book, in an article, in a blog, in an advertisement, or in something you are listening to write down the phrase.

Full phrase

Here you need to remember that you shouldn't write just one word, write down the entire phrase, or you can even write down the entire sentence containing that word or phrase. This way, you will have a notebook full of phrases and sentences that you may use anytime, not just individual words. You'll be training yourself to speak in phrases instead of word by word.

If you're watching a movie, for example, you might hear a character say, "He fell head over heels for that girl!" You may understand 'falling head over heels, in the literal sense, as tumbling forward. So, you may get confused. Then when you look it up in an idiomatic dictionary, you learn that one meaning of "head over heels " is to be madly in love. This can be with a person or even a thing. Even if you had previously memorized the words 'head', 'over', and 'heels', separately on some vocabulary lists, you still might not understand what the character in the movie is saying. But since you wrote down the phrase, you now know a new expression you can use in different situations.

Context

Let's say someone describes their neighbor's pet by saying, "She was a bad cat." It's quite a simple sentence, but you write it down in your notebook. Every time you review, you read that complete statement. By doing that, you are acquiring free grammar - she was. You know that this was something that was true in the past, not 'she is', which would mean the cat was still around.

You're also getting some free ideas about word usage. The word disgusting also conveys the meaning - bad and unacceptable. But we don't usually say "she was a disgusting cat", even though the meaning is correct. In normal spoken English, we don't usually use that word to describe a cat. This is not what you would learn from studying the dictionary meaning of disgusting. You learn it only by studying a phrase.

Source

Whenever you write down a phrase, don't forget to write the source. If you read it in a newspaper article, in some finance news, put that down. If you come across a new phrase in a YouTube video, write down the name of the channel and the topic of the video in front of the phrase. If you hear some new word from a speaker, write down the name of the speaker.

That is going to trigger your memory. You will be able to recall how the word was used and in what context. You'll begin to learn when to use certain phrases and words and when not. This way, you'll begin to get a feeling about what is correct and how to put sentences together.

Don't write the translation

A very essential thing to remember here is, never write the translation for the word or phrase in your native language. We have already discussed the reason above.

Keep Reviewing

Just maintaining a "Phrase bank" is not enough. To get a significant improvement in your speaking ability, it is essential, that you use those phrases in your day-to-day speaking. For that, it is very important that you keep revisiting and reviewing your collection every day.

3- day Exercise- Improve your Vocabulary using movies

Day 1

Day 1 involves the longest commitment in terms of time as compared to the other two days. However, in terms of effort, it is the most relaxing and entertaining day. You just need to choose your favorite movie or tv show and play it on. Watch the entire movie. The things you need to take care of, try to understand the movie thoroughly. As much as you can. For this, you may even turn on the subtitles, in English or your native language, as per your convenience. You may also lower the speed, and replay certain parts if you feel comfortable doing so. Here, I would recommend watching the movie alone, not with your spouse, kids, siblings, or friends, you may turn up frustrating people. That's all for the first day.

Day 2

Step 1: Select a scene (maybe the first scene of the movie or your favorite scene) or a clip of 2 to 3 minutes. Play it along with the subtitles in ENGLISH.

Step 2: As you watch & listen to the scene and read along with the subtitles, in a notebook, pen down the words, phrases, idioms, and slang you come across. Specifically, those which are new to you.

Step 3: Use your paperback dictionary or your web dictionary to write down the meanings of those words against them. NOTE: don't write the translation in your native language and don't try to memorize it.

Step 4: Watch the entire scene again. This time you will observe that you notice those words more than before. You may even be able to understand a few. Don't bother if you don't comprehend all.

Step 5: Take a glance at your vocab list, just a quick one. Don't try to memorize.

Step 6: Watch the scene again keeping the subtitles ON. You will be surprised to find that you are able to understand most of the words now.

Repeat steps 5 & 6, several times. This entire exercise will take not more than 25- 30 minutes.

Day 3

Repeat watching the same scene. This time without any subtitles.

Step1: Play the scene without subtitles, as you listen to the actors speak those words & phrases, you will be able to grasp most of them.

Step 2: Move to your vocabulary list, and review it quickly.

Step 3: Play the scene again, this time you might be able to understand almost all the words. Amazing! You will feel awesome

Step 4: Repeat steps 4-5-6-7 times. The exercise will take just 15-20 minutes.

This is an amazing technique that will help you internalize these words and that too subconsciously, without memorizing or cramming. The words will automatically flow out in your writing or speaking.

TRY IT OUT! Although it might take over a month to finish the movie like this, it may also feel overwhelming at times yet it has amazing results which make it worth trying.

Remember, “if you do what you always did, you get what you always got”, Albert Einstein. If you think your old traditional methods have not been helping you to improve your vocabulary, try this technique today itself.

CHAPTER SIXTEEN

Perfection Through Repetition

"The quality of your practice determines the caliber of your performance."- Robin Sharma

Often English learners know a lot of grammar and vocabulary. Still, when it comes to speaking, they struggle to understand the meaning of what is being said to them, they translate vocabulary, and they analyze tenses in their heads. As a result, their English sounds synthetic and robotic. The only reason is that they have not trained themselves for mastery. Mastering English means learning English to the level where speaking and understanding English both are subconscious and automatic.

For example, let's talk about the past tense. You know a lot about past tense. you have studied and solved grammar exercises to get perfect scores. You know all about past continuous, past perfect, past perfect continuous tense. Congratulations! But then, why do you still make mistakes when you speak? Knowing past tense is different from being able to use it subconsciously and automatically in real conversations. You need a refined skill, not mere knowledge (chapter- 4). The problem is that you learn a lot of things but you forget them or you remember the basic idea but you can't use it because:

- You haven't mastered it.
- You haven't learned it deeply.
- You haven't practiced like native speakers.
- You practiced like an English student.

Repetition is the key to Mastery.

In my Turbo English Mastery Program, the students train themselves. They achieve perfection through repetition. How does a professional batsman master the game and continue to improve with every match he plays? Suppose he practices 300 balls every day. He would practice just one shot. If it's cover-drive, it will be only cover-drive for all 300 balls. And that is why when he plays the actual match everything seems so natural as if he is hitting the ball subconsciously. So, you have to practice, repeat and repeat until it gets into your muscle memory.

How the brain makes memories?

The first thing to understand is how our brain creates a memory. Information comes in through our senses—our ears, eyes, skin, nose, or tastebuds. Once the information comes in, it needs to get encoded—and by that, I mean, it needs to be 'written' in a language the brain understands so it can be stored and remembered.

Here we make a distinction between short-term memory and long-term memory. Short-term or what is also called 'working' memory is the holding area where information stays when it first comes in: For example, someone tells us his phone number and we repeat it back keeping it in working memory- it's like a whiteboard you scribble on in your brain for your incoming information. Short-term memory lasts for a few minutes. It is when short-term memory makes the shift to long-term memory. Long-term memory can last days, weeks, years, or forever.

How does information move from short-term memory to long-term memory? How to store the English we learn in long-term memory?

Often psychologists think of memory as organized in 'chunks'- basic interconnected units. Each chunk can be described by its 'activation', which means, how easily that chunk can be retrieved from memory.

For instance, your name forms a chunk in your memory; it contains very high activation — if you are awakened even in the middle of the night and asked, "What is your name?", you'd be able to reply fairly quickly. On the other hand, if you had to remember the name of your first-grade teacher, that answer would likely be harder to come up with, because its activation is lower.

The activation or the retrieval of a chunk is influenced by three different factors:

- **Practice**: Number of times a chunk has been used in the past
- **Recency**: how recently a chunk has been used
- **Context**: what's there in the person's focus of attention

It's a common saying, that "practice makes perfect". In fact, the more you practice a piece of information, the more likely you are to remember it: the activation of a chunk is dependent on the amount of practice that it has received. That's part of the reason why your name is so much more familiar than that of your first-grade teacher, it has received a lot more practice through repetition.

The second factor that affects activation is recency, or how far away in the past you've used a chunk. This also affects how well you remember information. To explain it, something that has been used very recently possesses a higher activation than a piece of information that you've not used for a while (for example, the name of your first-grade teacher).

Other than practice and recency, the third-factor activation depends upon, is context. As I said earlier those chunks are interconnected memory units. The connection between two chunks is called *association*. If I say the word Paris and ask you to say what words come to mind once you hear it, you'll come up with France, Ratatouille, Eiffel Tower, or Napoleon. The words are strongly related to Paris, and when Paris gets within the focus of attention (that is, you've just heard it or read it), it spreads activation to other chunks related to it. The foremost active chunk in your memory is the one selected as your first response; the subsequent most active chunk is going to be your second response, and so on. (Note that the associations between concepts are extremely personal and depend on previous experience: a French person may have totally different associations with the word *Paris* than an American.)

The concept of association is tremendously important in psychology. It forms the basis of learning and problem-solving. It allows us to have a relevant conversation. But how does context affect the retrieval of data from memory? When something in our current environment (the smell and taste of a cookie) is strongly related to a piece in our memory, it spreads activation to that chunk making it more active.

RAR

So, the technique that can move the English words phrases, and grammar we learn from short-term memory to long-term memory is called **RAR**, Repetition, Association, Review

Repetition

Repetition is the most familiar learning & practicing tool --everyone has memorized facts or vocabulary words by repeating them, and some have improved basketball free-throw shooting or playing piano scales through practice. *Repetition creates the strongest learning*—and most learning—both implicit (like tying your shoes) and explicit (multiplication tables) relies on repetition (Chapter-3). So here in the Turbo English Mastery program, we have a strategical method of repetition.

Association

Association is the ability of a piece of information to tap into a neural connection that already exists. It's the equivalent of already having a file folder for the new learning to go into. For example, if I read a series of ten numbers aloud and asked you to recollect them and say them back to me typically you'd find this a difficult task. But if the ten numbers also happened to be your telephone number, then the task would be easy, and if I asked you a year later what the numbers were, you'd still be ready to give them to me because they were already a part of a previous neural connection.

Do you remember when you were a young kid how you repeated words/phrases and even sentences that you heard around you from your mother, family members caretakers, or even neighbors? That is how you have acquired your native language through repetition and when this repetition is in context with an association, it makes learning, and language learning even simpler.

Review.

You must keep on reviewing the information and learning. Practicing every day as a ritual is a must.

How to use RAR?

Exercise 1

1. Pick an Audio that is 10 minutes long.
2. You can listen to the audio along with text or the English subtitles to understand better.
3. Listen to it a few times- morning, lunchtime, after returning from work, at bedtime, and whenever you get a chance.

Let the English wash over your body and brain.

Rules:

- The mindset should be mastery.
- Don't try to memorize anything
- Just try to focus and understand the context.
- Let it go deeper. You are planting a seed in your brain and nurturing it with repeated listening.
- Be relaxed, cheerful, and energized. Keep a smile on your face.

Four stages of understanding in your brain:

I. There are some words which you don't know at all. A few words that you understand but not a hundred percent. You may have to look them up in the dictionary, even then you might forget them.
II. You know it a little bit. Sometimes you forget. You know them, but not 100%.
III. You know it completely, understand it whenever you read or listen to it, but passively.
IV. Active: you can actually use it quickly, easily, effortlessly, and subconsciously whenever you speak or write.

Point to remember: Move to the next audio only when you have reached and mastered stage III for the previous audio.

Exercise 2- Listening and speaking

DAY 1:

Choose an audio for practice. Listen to it several times just as in exercise 1. Concentrate on just learning vocabulary Write down the phrases. Find the meanings. Understand the context. Play with text.

DAY 2:

Try to understand the audio completely without the text.

DAY 3:

Practice the audio using Imitation Technique (chapter- 14). Keep working on your pronunciation as well. Play a sentence, pause, shout. Focus on pronunciation. Copy speaker's rhythm, tone, and enunciation. If you feel self-conscious, do it behind closed doors, until you feel confident enough. Practice it a multitude of times. Don't forget to control your emotions by reprogramming the anchors (Chapter- 11).

DAY 4:

If you feel comfortable, play 2 sentences & repeat with emotions. If not, you may continue imitating one sentence at a time.

DAY 5:

Return to listening and understanding

Why Repetitive listening?

- You don't memorize, you are internalizing the phrases and grammar.
- You completely understand what you hear.
- You are mastering the skill of English like a batsman.
- You develop a "Sense of correctness."

- You are acquiring English naturally & subconsciously.

How many times to repeat the audio?

Each audio should be repeatedly listened to for at least a week. Every day it should be listened to at least 7 times. 49 times a week. Maybe 100 times a week. The more the better.

Patricia A. Duff, Professor of Language and Literacy Education, University of British Columbia, mentions, "Repetition is viewed as a way of providing learners greater access to language forms-for example, by repeating forms for learners (Chaudron, 1977) -and as a means of enabling learners to develop automaticity in the target language as they proceed from highly controlled language use to more automatic or spontaneous production of internalized forms."

Another great way to improve your listening and speaking skills is, the "shadowing technique ", but lots of people don't know about it.

Shadowing Technique

In the shadowing technique try listening to the audio-video content freely, enjoy listening to the speaker, and enjoy the English language musically. Like music, every language has its rhythm and melody. The speed and the stress constitute the rhythm and the intonation, the enunciation, constitutes the melody. The intonation is the rise and fall of the voice, the volume, and the speed of the speaker which makes speaking expressive and can help a person to understand the emotions behind your words.

This technique is called the shadowing technique because as the shadow moves along with your body, in this exercise you have to repeat the speaker as soon as possible. You're acting like an "echo" or a "shadow" of the speaker. Remember that you're not listening to the audio, stopping it, and then repeating it. You're repeating it *as* you're listening. Shadowing was popularised by ***Alexander Arguelles***, who is a "polyglot".

How are we going to do this?

1. **Select any English content**: Choose any easy and enjoyable audio or video from the wide range of podcasts, audiobooks, or YouTube videos.
2. **Listen to the audio first.** Shadowing is most effective when you understand the content before you repeat it. So, if you choose from podcast YouTube videos and audiobooks you have already gone through then it's better. Check that you understand all the key vocabulary.
3. **Shadow the audio with a transcript.** This is the easier version of shadowing: speaking with the audio while also reading a transcript. This helps you to *see* the words as you're repeating them. If you're a beginner or lower-intermediate English learner, this is a great option for you.
4. **Shadow without a transcript.** If you're a bit more advanced, you can jump straight to this step and do shadowing without the transcript.
5. **Start right away**: Turn on the audio and try repeating the speaker as soon as possible. Don't wait for the speaker to complete the sentence, speak almost at the same time as the speaker.
6. **Use your body**: Alexander Arguelles, suggests that you do your shadowing while you're walking outside. Walk outside, briskly, maintain good posture, repeat what you hear loudly, and mimic the mannerisms of the speaker- body language, vocal variety, expressions everything. Just think of yourself as an actor preparing for the auditions.

To some of you, walking quickly outside might seem strange, but the idea is to keep the oxygen flowing to your brain, making you more alert, and increasing your brain functionality. "Motions set your emotions"

How to add these activities to your life?

Should you do all of them every day? If yes, at what time of the day? In the morning or at night. What if you don't have time to do them at all?

All these questions might be flustering your mind. Let me share my learning routine that's absolutely doable for people like us. If you follow this routine your spoken English will progress, while still, having time left for other areas of your life. While it's best to focus on this activity, you *can* also do this while you're doing other things. For example, you can do it in the car on your commute to work, while you're out jogging, or even while you're having a bath. I encourage you to listen to English during such activities it will allow you to learn English speaking without spending your free time.

Is the shadowing technique effective?

Shadowing is a useful technique for developing speaking fluency in English. It especially helps in improving pronunciation, intonation, and rhythm. Several studies have shown that it can be an effective way to improve speaking skills. For example, in one experiment at the National Taiwan University, researchers found that including a shadowing technique significantly improved students' intonation, fluency, word pronunciation, and overall pronunciation.

According to researchers, shadowing is effective for developing listening comprehension, the ability to produce speech, the ability to learn new words, and metacognitive monitoring skills for language.

It has been proven that "shadowing' can be an effective activity in a variety of language teaching and learning environments. The best part is, that it's an amazing way to practice and improve your English speaking even when you don't have a practice partner.

Remember, rehearsals come before results even in the dictionary. Repetitions are the only method of rehearsals. Repetitions put the actions in your muscle memory to an extent that they become subconscious and automatic.

CHAPTER SEVENTEEN

SUBCONSCIOUS GRAMMAR WITH THE GRAMMAR STORIES.

Grammar is a piano I play by ear since I seem to have been out of school the year the rules were mentioned. "- Joan Didion, American writer, 1934

Most of the students who come to me are shocked, when I tell them, "You don't need to study Grammar to master spoken English." They believe that Grammar study is the key to fluent English speaking. English learners are wired by the traditional teaching methods, that they cannot learn English without studying grammar rules.

In school, I was told by my English teacher, that you must study grammar if you wish to be good at English. I still have the "Wren & Martin", which was the bible of English Grammar for us, and a thick register in which my tuition master made me write all the tenses, their rules, with their examples in Hindi as well, and various translations of several sentences in different tenses. When I joined various English-speaking classes, everywhere there were Grammar drills, Grammar textbooks to be solved. For years I studied and focused on Grammar rules.

Did that strategy help? Was I able to speak English easily, quickly, fluently, and subconsciously? Did I get the results I was seeking? Even my English tutor wasn't able to speak in English, although he was extremely well versed in Grammar. He knew all about English. He made me learn how to learn English. I wasn't able to use English.

English speaking is not knowing English. It is using English as you know it. In fact, it is "DOING ENGLISH", just like you do any other activity to practice and master it.

From the perspective of Grammar in English learning, 3 leading questions arise

First, why are certain constructions learnable and others not? What is it about these constructions which makes them so difficult to acquire?

Second, in considering input requirements, can we say that adult learners can take advantage of metalinguistic information about the language and negative input? Do adults differ from child learners in the English input requirements?

Finally, is focal attention required for the acquisition of the syntax and the phonological rules of English? Do we need to notice to learn, or can we subconsciously learn Grammatical aspects?

The Monitor Model by Dr. Stephen Krashen (Chapter-5), claims that adult second-language performers have two means of internalizing the rules of a target language:

(1) **language *acquisition***, which is primarily subconscious, is not influenced by overt teaching or error correction, and is very similar to primary language acquisition in children;

(2) **language *learning***, which involves the conscious representation of pedagogical rules, is influenced by teaching and error detection.

The model hypothesizes that learning is available to the adult second-language performer only as a Monitor—that is, people use conscious grammar only to alter the output of the acquired system.

Grammar study hurts your English speaking.

In Chapter 3 we understood that Grammar is important for learning English. But we need to understand that grammar is not a stand-alone subject.It is the study of the behavior of words which are reflections of changes in the experiences and sounds of words. A student who seeks to get fluency in English; has to study the three tenses of English, its rules, and know, how to apply them in sentences. For most people, using 'grammar' in real conversation only leads to trouble. Let us understand WHY?

1. Analysis

When you analyze each part of your sentence from a Grammatical perspective, as if you are solving a problem in Maths or Physics, you become confused. Just imagine a football player playing on the field, trying to use Physics- friction, kinetic force, or the speed of the wind. Would he be able to play the game smartly?

2. Thinking about Grammar

You think about grammar, only grammar all the time. Is it past perfect tense, present continuous tense, or is it the first conditional/ which infinitive to use? When you are writing something in English you have all the time in the world to review and edit, everything you have penned down. You can visit it multiple times and change the structure of the sentences. You can erase your mistakes. You don't have to write fast.

But when someone asks you something and you have to respond in English you don't have time to think. You can't keep thinking about the present perfect continuous tense. You have to respond instantly, spontaneously. You don't have time to apply rules of prepositions, phrasal verbs, comparatives, and everything else which you have learned in an English classroom.

Linguists like Dr. Stephen Krashen suggest a more natural approach. He mentions, "Learning a language doesn't require extensive use of conscious grammatical rules and does not require tedious grammar drills."

3. It makes you conscious

Tell me are you interested in knowing how the plane flies? Or you are interested in traveling and reaching your destination. Are you interested in using the mobile or are you interested in knowing how a mobile functions? This is something that you need to understand in the context of English too. Are you interested in speaking English or do you want to know about English? When you know too much and you try applying all the information it makes you conscious. You put conscious effort to apply the grammar rules to accuracy.

Author Laura Batternik, Ph.D., a neurologist at the University of Oregon. "You can think of that intuitively—when you're speaking English you don't need to consciously remember all the grammar rules, you're just following them."

4. Slow, hesitant & fabricated speech

When you constantly analyze & think about grammar. You become conscious and your language is paralyzed. The speech which flows from your mouth will be slow and hesitant. Each and every sentence you speak will be fabricated and unnatural. Even if you speak correct English, it will kill the natural conversation and frustrate the listener.

So, should we stop learning Grammar? Is Grammar a waste of time? Definitely not. Grammar is the main feature in both written and spoken English. It allows you to make your message clearly understood by the listener. The shift has to be in the way you learn grammar. The way I make my students learn grammar in my '**Turbo English Mastery**" Program is - *subconsciously.*

Subconscious Grammar

Imagine you have a friend who is fluent in English or he may be a native speaker. "One way to clarify mental or competence grammar is to ask a friend a question about a sentence," Pamela J. Sharpe writes in "Barron's How to Prepare for the TOEFL IBT." "Your friend probably won't know why it's correct, but that friend will know *if* it's correct. So, one of the features of mental or competence grammar is this incredible *sense of correctness* and the ability to hear something that *'sounds odd'* in a language."

Subconscious grammar learning is based on this "*Sense of Correctness*". This is the method through which native speakers use to learn and master English grammar. They do not study grammar or learn phrases. They use natural methods to identify what *'sounds right.'*

This is how you have learned your first language. You don't think about verb conjugations or tenses while speaking. When a person speaking in your native language commits a mistake you instantly feel that grammar itch when you hear a not-quite-right sentence.

A new study from the University of Oregon found that even if you don't consciously recognize a grammar error, your brain still realizes something is wrong and sends out a negative signal.

Your Subconscious Mind is responsible for automatic responses. The subconscious brain is way faster than your conscious brain. It can process large quantities of information gathered through your 5 senses and can send them back to your brain within the blink of an eye. So, trust the natural and subconscious way of learning grammar and allow your grammar to improve automatically.

How to learn Grammar Subconsciously? - Grammar Stories

If vocabulary words and phrases are the building blocks of a language, Grammar acts as a glue to put them together, so that your sentences are structured properly and make sense when you talk.

When you are meeting new people or visiting new places, the last thing you wish is to be misunderstood by the people. Grammar is important for your social and professional life.

A simple technique that I use to make my students learn grammar subconsciously is the 'Grammar Stories'. These are simple short stories in which we alter the time frame due to which the grammar gets altered. We use this to create several versions of the same story.

When you read or listen to these innovative reconstructions, you learn grammar subconsciously without focussing on tenses, conjugations, and other things. Most importantly, these stories are easy and enjoyable (Chapter 14). The noticeable thing here is that by understanding the context of the stories, you absorb the spoken grammar skills naturally and automatically.

The Grammar stories technique is based on the TPRS learning system- Teaching Proficiency through Reading & Story-telling. The teaching of language through reading and storytelling is a method that uses different resources for language teaching, providing comprehensible input information in imaginary or real situations derived from students' social context and their cognitive and affective needs. A study was done at the Catholic University of Cuenca, an extension of Cañar. The results show that the students obtained better results in the measures of vocabulary acquisition, and the students perceive that the strategies derived from the method were of great support to acquiring vocabulary in English.

Benefits

1. You don't require to study and think about tenses, conjugations, and other abstract grammar rules.
2. They are relaxing and fun, so the affective filter is low. You absorb the grammar naturally and subconsciously.
3. You acquire meaning and memorable English through the context stories.

4. You will be able to USE the grammar so acquired correctly without thinking and analyzing.
5. You learn grammar like native speakers as the babies do.
6. You set yourself free from the chains of abstract grammar rules and knowledge.
7. Most importantly, you develop the "*sense of correctness*", you instantly realize the correct grammar because it will "*sound right*" to you, just like your native language.

The Rules

1. Audio only

It is important that you use audio versions only. Remember listening is the key to speaking. If the target is to learn spoken grammar skills, it should be learned with ears.

2. Do not analyze

Zip up your analytical brain. There is no need to identify linguistic grammar rules. You should not analyze the tenses, conjugations, or other changes that occur due to the change in the time frame. Don't be bothered whether it is simple past or past perfect and so on. Just understand the context and enjoy the story. Let the English wash over you.

3. The third 'E'

Remember the 3 Es of listening- Easy, Enjoyable, Endless. You need to listen to these grammar stories several times. Just listen and try to understand the context and meaning of each version. Listen to each one 7 times every day for seven days.

When you learn grammar like this, using the grammar stories, you are training yourself as an athlete. You are acquiring the grammar knowledge automatically and you will use the correct grammar subconsciously.

CHAPTER EIGHTEEN

Real English-Learn from Authentic Materials

Do not use textbooks to learn English. Aside from a focus on explicit grammar, textbooks overload you with vocabulary in a way that lowers your confidence, until you have the best memory. That is why you find it hard to understand and when you speak people look confused.

Too much Vocabulary

Textbook chapters typically have at least 20 different words used just once or twice in a text passage. Very few of these new words recur. As a result, you are exposed to a lot of meanings, yet only a few grammatical structures at a time according to the chapter's grammar focus. This does not help comprehension—the *sine qua non* of language acquisition—and restricts you from creating a mental representation of the language. Instead, you require to limit the vocabulary, recycle the words often, and unleash grammatical structures as needed.

Formal English

Textbooks focus on formal conversations; they rely on written dialogues that are completely unnatural. This is the form that is mostly used in writing not speaking. A communicative approach does not mean planning for paired speaking activities, such as ordering lattes at a cafe. In fact, modern language training eliminates that kind of role-playing in the classroom.

Unnatural Pronunciation

Traditional textbook teaching methods teach you the dictionary pronunciation of English words. Such activities use strange rhythms and the pronunciation is completely synthetic. Students who learn English through traditional methods find it difficult to understand real conversations. In real life, the natives contract, shrink, diminish, and overlap many sounds. Such as how-ya-doing, nice-ta-meetcha, gonna, wassup. Even the advanced textbook learners struggle to understand and communicate in the real world.

Idioms

Idioms are phrases that have a meeting different from individual words. They are dependent on cultural references. It's difficult to understand them logically. For example, you hear your American colleague say, "I *have pulled out all the stops* for the presentation." The idiom means – to make your best efforts, reserve nothing, and do each and everything possible. This idiom is in reference to organ stops, which are pulled out to turn on each set of sounds in a pipe organ. When all stops are pulled out, the organ will play all variations of its sounds at once, therefore being as loud as possible. You will rarely find the phrase in textbooks.

Hence proving that textbooks are ineffective. So we need to use real and authentic materials.

What are authentic materials?

In the Asian Conference on Education 2017, authentic materials were identified as "materials which are created and used for the social purpose of the native speakers. Some examples of authentic materials are a magazine, maps, news, TV show, newspaper, and poster, they can also be in the form of listening materials such as radio shows and songs, and visual materials like TV shows and movies. Authentic materials are regarded as beneficial tools in teaching English in EFL countries since they reflect the naturalness of the language, trigger learners' motivation, contain cultural content, and improve the communicative competence." The authentic materials are real materials that exist in the real world of the target language, are used in their daily life, and are not produced for teaching purposes

In these, you are exposed to a wide net of language without the cognitive demand for new meanings and build mental representation more effectively. We have already discussed these materials in *Chapter 14* under the heading: 'The best English listening activities.'

Benefits of using Authentic materials.

- **Immersion:** you are keeping yourself surrounded by the language used by the native speakers. In this way, you submerge yourself in real English. This is how the babies learn. (chapter-9) This is how you learned your first language.
- **Authentic:** you make sure that you are using the English which is used in the real world by natives in real-life conversations. That will give you a better understanding and command of spoken English.
- **Communicative Competence:** Real-life materials can increase learners' communicative competence. A study was done by

Purcell-Gates, Degener, Jacobson, and Soler in 2002. The result shows that authentic materials improve learners' literacy development. It indicates that using authentic materials and authentic activities in the classroom give a better impact on the literacy of adult learners. It is argued that the learners are getting used to reading and writing more complex text outside the classroom after the teacher introduced authentic materials.

- **Learn the culture of the target language.** Rogers and Medley (1988) further add that authentic materials are resourceful materials to learn the culture of the target language. They contain cultural information which may benefit the learners to increase their awareness of different cultures. You learn idioms and phrases which are related to the culture. Through materials such as TV shows or magazines, students can learn the culture or the habit of the people in the target language which can satisfy their curiosity.

When you listen to real English materials, you learn, absorb and acquire the natural English as it is used by the natives. You will understand fast English, accents, idioms, and phrases as soon as you hear them. This will help you understand the series, TV shows, and movies about which you felt really frustrated. You will enjoy them without any stress.

CHAPTER NINETEEN

EFFECTIVE READING FOR ENGLISH MASTERY

"Reading and writing don't inevitably go together. You read without learning a thing about writing, grammar or spelling, although you certainly can't learn anything about writing grammar, or spelling unless you read"- Frank smith

Reading is one of the best activities you can do every day to improve your English. Studies have consistently shown that those who read more show more literacy development.

Stephen Krashen says language acquisition is driven by "comprehensible input". Comprehensible input means content that can be understood by someone despite them not understanding every word and sentence in it. To get this comprehensible input in English, you have to be *exposed* to it. So, one of the ways through which we provide English input to our brains is listening. However, another effective way to get lots of English input is to read. Reading in English is an immensely effective English-learning activity. Reading results in language and literacy development.

Power of Reading

There is a multitude of benefits of reading *in general.* It enhances your critical thinking skills, develops your concentration, and triggers your imagination. According to a new study presented at the annual meeting of the Radiological Society of North America (RSNA), reading may even slow down memory loss & can preserve structural integrity in the brains of older people. But in addition to all that, reading in English can be used as an effective way to learn English.

It improves your vocabulary

It can be difficult to remember and recall all the English words and phrases you learn owing to the forgetting curve.

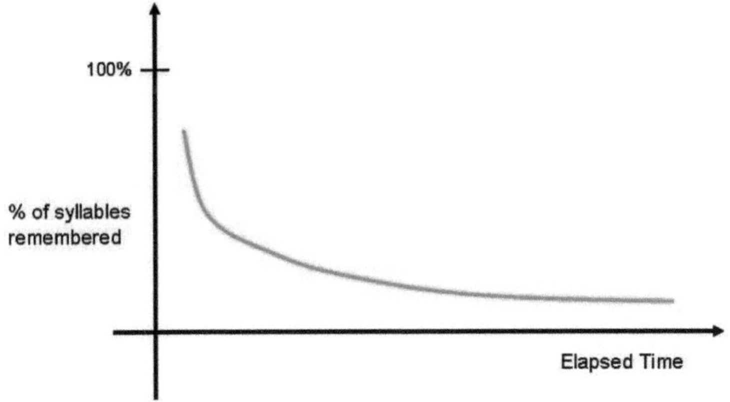

Ebbinghaus forgetting curve. The more time that goes by, the more we forget. (Image from Nheise at English Wikibooks.)

It's even more difficult if you're learning the words *out of context.* That "75 important English idioms that will make you speak like a native." list might be attractive, but you're probably not going to remember all of them. Reading is a savior because it provides you context for new words. You are not only able to understand what the word is, but also how to use it. Lots of research show that reading affects English learning positively. It improves students' reading, vocabulary, and grammar achievement.

It improves your grammar

Reading also helps you get a 'sense of correctness' of grammar. (Chapter 17) By observing how English is used, you develop a subconscious understanding of how it works. Indeed, research suggests that reading widely helps improve both grammar knowledge and the accurate usage of grammar.

It improves your comprehension skills

Reading English books is just not meant for advanced English students. But reading may help you to become an advanced level student. Reading in English improves your English comprehension skills. More specifically, reading widely helps you get better at *understanding what you read* and *helps you read faster*. Several empirical studies and synthesis of extensive reading have concluded that extensive reading has a positive impact on language learning in second and foreign language settings. They prove the positive impacts of extensive reading on all three areas- the reading comprehension, reading rate, and vocabulary acquisition

So reading is the most important fundamental skill a person can acquire. However, it seems to be a big problem for students because most of them find English reading difficult and lack the motivation in doing so. if you find reading in English a bit painful, just keep doing it. You'll get better, and it'll make it easier to do in the future.

It improves your attitude towards learning English

A much more important factor is your *attitude* towards the language. Let us understand the relation between students' reading comprehension and attitudes towards language learning. Gardner

(1980: 267) defines attitudes as 'the sum total of a man's instincts and feelings, prejudice or bias, preconceived notions, fears, threats, and convictions about any specified topic'. In the English learning context, a positive attitude boosts the process of learning; the negative one hampers the learning process.

Generally, attitudes concerning language acquisition can be divided into three types: attitude towards the language, attitude towards the native speaker of the language, and attitude towards language learning. If students have a positive attitude towards the process of learning a language, they will enjoy more the lessons and, as a result, they can catch up on more knowledge and skill in the language. Reading in English can improve your attitude.

It was found in a study that students who were given extensive reading activities reported that they felt more comfortable with English, gave more intellectual value to reading, and felt less anxious and fearful about the language.

It gives you unlimited input

Sometimes getting stuck in the middle of the conversation is not due to a lack of English-speaking skills or grammar information overload but it might be due to the fact that you simply don't have much knowledge or absolutely NO knowledge about the topic. So first you need to know "what you want to say". We understand that large amounts of "comprehensible input" are an essential requirement for learning a language. Just as podcasts provide tonnes of language input, so does reading. If you want lots of exposure to English content in a relatively quick time, reading is ideal. "The quality of your thoughts is determined by the quality of your reading"- James Clear. So, read English regularly. English reading can make a huge impact—it is one of the most effective ways to get acquainted with the language and amplify your learning.

Free Voluntary Reading

Dr. Krashen introduced the concept of "free voluntary reading." The hypothesis claims that reading results in an increase in literacy and language development when reading appears to be effortless, and we are so focused on the message that we don't even notice that it contains language (grammar and vocabulary) that we have not yet acquired. For English readers, optimal acquisition happens when readers are not even aware that the text is in English. It also states that "hard work" and suffering are proof that literacy development is not taking place.

It doesn't mean, everything that is fun is good for you, but as far as literacy development is concerned, the path of pleasure is the most trusted. The focus should not be on the "classics." Rather, the focus must be on the literature that English learners will find interesting and comprehensible. Depending on the age and background of the students, this could mean comic books, magazines, romance novels, mysteries, and newspapers.

You need to understand that:

(1) Language acquisition occurs most efficiently when we are so involved in the message that we "forget" it is in English, or that it contains aspects of English that we have not yet acquired.

(2) For reading to best stimulate English language development, it should appear to be effortless.

(3) Readers acquire best when they are not aware that they are improving. They are only aware of the content of what they have read.

(4) The more we check comprehension, the lesser readers understand and the less they acquire

Sustained silent reading

In SSR, a few minutes each day is devoted to recreational reading, usually between 5 and 15. It is more effective to do a little each day than to devote large amounts of time once or twice a week to do free reading. The goal of SSR is to develop a taste for reading, to stimulate the once-reluctant reader to read more outside of school.

Rather than forcing reading, and possibly making it distasteful, small doses are much more likely to work. It is not the actual time reading during SSR that counts, it is the desire to read more, that counts. Thus, SSR is not for very advanced readers.

Self-selected reading

Self-selected reading programs were popular in the United States in the 1950s. In self-selected reading, the entire class period is devoted to recreational reading, except for a small amount of time devoted to teacher-student conferences in which teachers discuss what the child reads, any problems that may have come up, and recommend additional reading.

Narrow reading

An interesting hypothesis is that narrow, rather than broad or wide reading, is more efficient for second language acquisition. This means the work of one author, one genre, or topic (e.g., only detective novels). Although we talk about reading here, the idea of narrow input must be applied to listening as well. Narrow reading will be more interesting, by definition, because it is restricted to what the reader really wants to read. It will be more comprehensible, because the reader will already have a great deal of background knowledge, and will gain more background knowledge by reading. Deep reading on any topic, will provide exposure to a tremendous amount of syntax and vocabulary that is used in other topics. Any technical field, for example, will use "subtechnical" vocabulary, words such as "function," "inference," "isolate," "relation," etc. (Cowan, 1974).

There is other evidence supporting the narrow reading idea. Lamme (1976) found that good readers in English as a first language tended to read more books by a single author and books from a series, for instance, they are the fans of Nancy Drew, the Hardy Boys, and Bobbsey Twins.

How you can read effectively?

The "free voluntary reading" concept can be utilized to make the most out of your reading activities.

1. Create time pockets for reading.

Make sure you set aside time to read directly—even making it directly a part of your English study schedule—will help ensure that you actually do it. Try to read a little bit every day, even if that's just 10-15 minutes.

2. Choose what you like.

Always choose English content that *interests you* so that you stay curious and motivated. The more you can satisfy your curiosity with your reading material, the more you will engage yourself in reading.

3. Choose as per your level.

If you choose something too difficult, or if you have to look into the dictionary after every 3 to 5 words, then it's clear you are not reading the content effortlessly. You might get frustrated or stressed. There is definitely no free reading hence no language acquisition. It's important to challenge yourself, but it's also important to not get frustrated. You should be able to understand between 85% and 90% of what you're reading. No understanding, no learning.

4. Recapitulate.

Thinking about what you're reading helps keep it from simply being a passive learning activity (chapter 14). You can write a summary of what you read in a reading journal to make it an active learning activity. You may also talk about it with your friends.

5. Read it anew.

"Reading is sowing. Rereading is harvesting"- Johnny Uzan. Don't abstain from reading something *again. There is nothing to feel bad about reading something afresh.* We often get much more out of something the second time around.

6. Don't stop for words as you're reading.

Finding new vocabulary and putting them in your vocabulary bank is a very good and most recommended exercise. But stopping every time, to look up a word, breaks your rhythm, it really ruins the experience. Instead, you may highlight or underline new words and when you are done reading at least a page or two, come back to them. That way, you can make a note of new words without losing your reading flow.

Reading is a vital activity for English learners. It does not only improve your English language skills but also enhances your literacy levels. It also helps give you some insight into English *cultures* as well. Making you comfortable with the language. The most effective English learning activity is the activity that you'll *enjoy* and that you'll spend time *doing.* Once you get the hang of the language, reading in English could be something you absolutely love. It can be *fun.* And at that point, you'll really see your English skills improve subconsciously.

CHAPTER TWENTY

English is for Communicative Competence

Why is English so important? Why must you learn this language?

To earn respect

"I wanted to change my profession. I had been working for a company for almost 7 to 8 years. After that, all my colleagues resigned one by one and got good jobs. Because of my poor English communication, I was scared to resign and go to another company. But finally, I made up my mind and started giving interviews. My first interview was at DHL logistic company. Three officials interviewed me and asked rapid questions. I didn't know how to answer in proper English. I was completely blank and petrified. The interviewer sent me out for a couple of minutes. But I didn't dare to go into that cabin again and left the place. I felt so humiliated. That day I realized the urgency of improving my English. After that, I joined many classes but unfortunately, they taught only grammar, and no speaking skills. Until I came across The Turbo English Mastery Program, which helped me to learn English naturally and subconsciously."- says, Lina Chandra, a software developer.

A person may be loveable in many ways, and he may possess excellent traits of character, but when he uses botched and broken English, we cannot think of him respectfully. Think about the people you are familiar with. Is there someone among them who uses poor English? Don't you look down upon them? You simply can't help it, no matter how much you like them.

I conducted a survey in which 200 people participated. 70.7 % of people believe that fluent English projects you as an intelligent intellectual and elite person. It earns you respect in society. They agree that people judge your education by the English you use. You may be a university graduate, but if your English is poor, you won't be credited for the education you've had. Although you may never be good at the grammar tests yet if you speak good English, you are considered educated.

To create an impression

Fluent English will help you make a good impression. It'll provide the means of calling attention to your abilities, which might be lying unnoticed because your speech didn't convey your potential to your employers. "It'll offer you a foothold over other employees within the daily competition for success". It is human psychology to be affected by what others think about us. When we create a good impression on others and that too without effort, naturally, it fills us with self-confidence and self-respect.

Travel places

It is quite apparent that English is a global language. So, when you are learning English, it is not just because you want to communicate with Americans or British or people from other English-speaking countries, you can be learning it for travel. For example, you go to Brazil, Germany, or Taiwan. If you don't know the local language of these places, in what language are you going to communicate with the people? For sure, English.

For business

Even for business. Most of the business interactions are between non-natives and non-native English speakers. So, if you want to become successful in business it's vital that you are able to speak English unless you are just doing business in your corner of the world. In the globalized world, more than ever it's essential to be able to connect your business to the other parts of the world.

Or maybe you are interested in politics. So, if you want to be able to get very far in your political career, of course, you have to have impressive English. So, it is not important to have an accent like native speakers. All that matters is to be able to speak clearly and confidently.

Internet usage

English is the key that you need to communicate with people from anywhere in the world. English can also open a whole new world, of different sources of information, for you. For example, the internet. Most of our information comes from the internet. Researchers from Tel Aviv University and the University of California at Berkeley have teamed up to gauge the nature of the relationship between linguistic patterns and Internet content.

Currently, about 70 percent of Internet content is in English, but only about 44 percent of Internet users are native English speakers. Worldwide, native Spanish speakers outnumber native English speakers, and the number of native Chinese speakers more than equals that of both groups.

English dominates online because it was established early on as the lingua franca of the wired world. If you have a good understanding of English, you will have all these sources of different information.

Bring a change

You can be the change you want to see in the world. English can help you do that. You can use your English to get different sorts of job opportunities. You could volunteer, and maybe you can get a job at an NGO. You can use your English every day with pride. Another thing you can do is help others by teaching them English. You can help other people to have the same discoveries, as you had, exploring a whole world, with a new perspective towards English.

There is a difference between 'speaking English' and 'speaking English and making sense'. Communication means that whatever you speak, be it in any language, it should make sense. The listener should be able to understand your point of view. People should comprehend - What you want to say. Communication is when you share your ideas, thoughts, values, suggestions, or perspectives in a clear, cohesive, organized, and confident way.

Remember (as proved by the Carnegie Institute of Technology) 85% of success in any field of business is due not to superior business knowledge, but to superior ability in influencing others. You need a command of English to achieve this. "You cannot possibly impress others until you have learned to express yourself."

Construct conversation- small talks

So far, we have discussed the exercises that you can do alone. Self-practice is an amazing exercise because you are not dependent on people this makes it possible for you to practice English consistently over practicing with a partner However, this exercise has one major advantage over self-practice it lets you practice your communication skills. One of the essential life skills- is public speaking. When you talk to people, you can pay attention you can learn how to make eye contact, how to use proper body language and facial expressions, and how to listen attentively most importantly you get a chance to practice making small talk in English.

What are small talks?

Small Talks are polite light informal conversations about not-so-important matters. In real life, there are some situations that require you to make small talk. For example- when you want to build rapport with someone or when you run into a friend or acquaintance or maybe you want to make some new contacts.

How to make 'small talk'?

So, there are three strategies that are going to help you to make 'small talk' in any situations

1. Asking open-ended questions

What do you mean by open-ended questions? Remember people enjoy talking about themselves, not only, we are our favorite subjects, also it is easier to discuss yourself than something you know little about. Open-ended questions generate an interesting and dynamic conversation and encourage the person to open up. For example, questions like

- What are you doing this weekend?
- What was the latest movie you watched and how was it?
- Do you play any musical instruments?
- Do you have an interest in music?
- What kind of music do you enjoy?
- Where are you from where is this city located?

So on and so forth for all these questions as you notice, are focused on the person whom you are talking to and people love themselves

2. *Active listening*

Remember you will be able to build much stronger connections if you pay attention to the conversation. “Simply listening very attentively was an important way of being helpful...... listen for the feelings and emotions behind the words.”- Carl R. Rojers.

Active listening means fully concentrating on what is being said rather than just passively ‘hearing’ the message of the speaker. Active listening involves listening with all senses and giving full attention to the speaker.

When the person speaking will notice how engaged you seem, he will usually feel more at ease and therefore communicate more easily, openly, and honestly. In addition, it must be easier to ask relevant questions and remember details to bring up later if you are not listening with one ear. So, it opens a room for further discussion.

3. *Show your enthusiasm*

To give full attention to the speaker, it is essential that the ‘active listener’ is also ‘visibly listening’ - otherwise the speaker may conclude that what they are talking about is uninteresting to the listener. That can be done by using both verbal and non-verbal messages such as maintaining eye contact, nodding your head and smiling, and agreeing by saying ‘Yes’ or simply ‘Mmm hmm’ to encourage them to continue.

All those small talks might not always be the most stress-free activity. However, if you think over it, with the right attitude you can actually have fun. You may take this as an opportunity to learn more about people you never know who you might meet and what they may have to share. So, embrace the chance of an amazing discussion.

Why do we sound boring?

Sometimes when we are making small talk conversations with people we may sound boring and people might lose interest in what we are speaking. So, what are the reasons? Why do we sound boring?

1. Hesitation

It's really impressive when you speak without hesitation. Too much hesitation distracts the listener from understanding your talk. You may link your ideas using connectors whenever you are about to hesitate, record your voice and analyze how many times you hesitate, add connectors in your talk, practice more and more, and instead of having fillers, you can take a pause

2. Long pauses or breaks

It becomes boring when you take long breaks in between when you are speaking. Noticeable pauses affect your speaking ability and may lead to a loss of interest in the person you are speaking with. To overcome this you need to practice speaking for longer time periods. You may practice through "self-analysis". Record your voice. Count and make a note of your long pauses. Try to remove them the next time you speak.

3. Repetition or self-correction

A very common mistake people do while speaking is, that they keep on correcting themselves when they speak. This again shows a lack of confidence. For example, after speaking a sentence if they realize that they have made a certain mistake in the usage of tenses, prepositions or the pronunciation, or other grammar rules, people tend to repeat that word, phrase, or sentence in the correct form.

What can you do? Try something new or form a new sentence every time you speak. Paraphrasing your sentence would help you to facilitate speaking so that you can extend your talk, without repetition. What is paraphrasing? Paraphrasing is- speaking the same words or sentences differently, using synonyms, or altering the grammatical structure. Suppose you want to repeat a sentence, you should try to change the grammatical structure of the sentence. For example, I have to say " I could not move out of the house because it was raining" So I can say this sentence like "the heavy rains prevented me from moving out of the house" note that I have changed the entire structure of the sentence, whereas the message remains the same.

4. Focusing on grammar

Remember your focus should be on your ideas and thoughts, not on translation and grammar. Let your ideas and thoughts flow. Imagine yourself as one of those English speakers whom you have been listening to in your practice days. Be consistent in practicing all the exercises we discussed in the preceding chapters.

5. Correct pronunciation

Pronouncing the words correctly is an important factor for English fluency. In case you feel that your speaking is more influenced by your native tongue, you definitely need to work on this. When you pronounce the word incorrectly, it drags the attention of the listener immediately. Pronunciation can be learned by listening to others and watching stuff online, which we have discussed already. Refer to the right source online to understand the pronunciation of a particular word.

6. Using complex vocabulary or idioms incorrectly

Usage of complex good vocabulary, phrases, and idiomatic expressions, no doubt decorate your speaking. Although sometimes we intentionally tend to add certain words, which makes it obvious and breaks the fluency of our speaking. Moreover, at other times when we add idiomatic expressions to our speaking, we must be crystal clear about their meanings. Otherwise, we may end up making a blunder. Do not try to forcefully use difficult words in talking and speaking use them subconsciously and correctly.

Win your listener- How to sound interesting?

As I said earlier, small talks may not be so interesting sometimes. So how can we add more details to our talk, so that the person listening to us can be more interested in speaking with us? Sometimes we find it difficult to add details to our ideas, even if we are very clear about our thoughts. But we cannot explain it properly. so let us understand how to add details to our conversation.

1. Answer with 5WH questions

Rudyard Kipling said, “I keep six honest serving men. They taught me all I knew; Their names are What and Why and When And How And Where and Who.” These questions help us to add details to your conversation and help us to speak at length without hesitation. For example,

1. What happened?
2. When did it happen?
3. Why did it happen?
4. Who else was involved?
5. Where did it happen?
6. How did it happen?

2. Give examples

Give relevant examples, analogies, and metaphors to support your perspective. It will help set the context and facilitate better understanding and set the ball rolling.

3. Tell stories

Stories can be utilized as a very effective tool. These can be tales or real-life experiences, derived from your life, other people's life, or general observations. Stories are engaging and help make the conversation more interesting, relevant, and meaningful.

4. Be specific

Whenever you are talking, try to be as specific as possible with Locations, names, Time & year, and emotional states. It creates a picture in the mind of the listener. The listener is able to visualize and feel whatever you are speaking and feel more connected and interested. Let us understand with the help of an example.

- One day when I moved out of my house, I saw my neighbor who was cleaning his car. I simply made it to my two-wheeler, without looking at him. The conversation would have cost another few minutes, as I was already running late.
- One fine Monday morning, when I rushed out of my house, I saw Mr. Whitman, scrubbing his XUV. I simply made it to my bike, hiding my face in the helmet. The conversation would have cost another 5 minutes, as I was already running late for my office.

Which description is more vivid and picturesque? If you speak in this way, I bet you are going to sound interesting.

Fluency killers- "The fillers"

Fluency in any language is speaking naturally, comfortably, and effortlessly. It is your ability to speak at a proper pace and with accuracy and proper expressions. It's your ability to speak without hesitation. Especially when the hesitation is to find the words, it distracts the listener from understanding your talk. Fillers "impede our ability to speak with power" and "become interrupters that detract from our message," says Cohen.

People may use speech fillers while they are hesitating to find a word or content such as uh, em, mm, which have no value in speaking. Steven Cohen, an assistant professor of communication at the University of Baltimore, says "Filler words "appear in every language and every culture." It's easy to understand why. When we need a moment to think, a quick interjection of an "um" feels like it can do wonders.

Noah Zandan, the chief executive at Quantified Communications, writes, 'However, relying too much on filler words can signal to the audience that a speaker is inarticulate or nervous.' One should try to minimize the use of filler words as much as possible as they lead to an impression of a lack of confidence.

Types of speech fillers

Filler words are used by the people to bridge the gap in speaking. there are three types of speech fillers.

Filler sounds – uh, ah, (signals a short delay) em, mm (signal a longer daily)

Filler words- so, but, like, actually, basically, literally

Filler phrase- you know, I mean, what I am trying to say is.

A great public speaker uses 1 filler@ per minute, but an average speaker uses 1 every 12 seconds or 5 fillers per @minute.

How to remove speech fillers?

1. Take a pause and think

Many speakers find themselves using speech fillers unconsciously. The good news is that you can turn your weakness into a strength. How? By replacing FILLERS with PAUSES. Research suggests, that the most conversational speeches consist of short 0.2 seconds, medium 0.6 seconds, and long over 1-second pauses. Great public speakers often pause for 2 to 3 seconds or even longer.

But for sure pauses are not easy to apply. For many speakers, even the smallest of pauses may seem like a long silence. The reason for this is, that our minds think faster than we speak. According to research, the average person speaks at a rate of 150 words per minute while a human brain thinks 400 words per minute and this rate may be as high as 1500 words per minute varying from person to person. Our thoughts race ahead of us. Well-placed pauses make you sound calm and collected and they help in three ways- 3Cs.

Collect your thoughts

If you lose track of your thoughts, a pause gives you time to get back on the track. As long as the pause is too long (not more than five seconds) the listener won't mind.

Calm your nerves

Taking a pause before starting a speech is especially a calming down exercise for people who are new to public speaking. The technique is useful in the middle of the conversation as well, if you find yourself getting confused, pause briefly to take a deep breath and reset. Obviously, your breath should not be audible or obvious to the listener.

Create suspense

Pauses aren't always used as a defense mechanism. If we use silence and pauses strategically, they may be used to

build suspense, emphasize a point or give the audience time to absorb certain information.

Just like with the filler words, pauses give a chance to take a break and think about what will come next. However, pauses make you sound confident and in control. Whereas the speech fillers are distracting and make you sound nervous.

2. Replace fillers with transitional words

Rather than saying uh, um, mm, you can instead use transitional words or phrases such as

For adding details,

- Another point I would like to say is that
- Another thing I want to mention as
- I would like to add
- In other words, we can say that
- Moreover, I think that
- Another point worth noting is
- Another factor to consider is
- Furthermore
- Besides
- In addition to
- Additionally

For mentioning examples (instead of just using like)

- For instance
- To exemplify
- To illustrate
- As an example

Instead of 'But' we can use words like

- although
- however
- besides
- alternatively
- in contrast to this

- on the other hand
- while

Instead of saying 'And' repeatedly

- likewise
- in the same way
- similar to or
- similarly

Practice more using these transitional words, especially at the time you are about to say mm/ uh, it would sound natural. Though, make sure that you use them rightly, use them in an appropriate context, and do not overuse them. Otherwise, it would create a negative impression. If you think you are making mistakes, use transitional words, use pauses instead.

3. Prepare your mind

Whenever given a chance to speak, it is always recommended to give your mind time to think. Take a pause for 10-20 seconds and organize your thoughts. Prepare your mind. Without this, you are more likely to be nervous. Which will affect your fluency. Always think strategically about what you want to say and how you want to organize it? While speaking be sure of yourself, do not doubt yourself.

4. Speak slowly not rapidly

Remember, 'pauses are punctuations for your talk',

Just as we use full stops and commas, when we write, treat pauses as punctuations, when we speak. Do not rush through what you have to say. Speak at a comfortable pace, keep your pace normal. Take pauses. It helps the listener to understand you better. If you speak fast you will end up using fillers after saying a few sentences.

5. Record your voice

The best strategy that works effectively is to record voice. you may use your phone to record your voice. Follow the following steps:

- Select any random topic and
- Keep speaking on the topic for 2 to 3 minutes.
- Now listen to your recorded voice
- Note down the following things -

a. The number of fillers,
b. Hesitation while speaking
c. Whether it was necessary to use a filler?
d. How did it affect your overall flow?

This will help you to analyze and do a 'self-evaluation' or 'self-analyses of your fluency. Moreover, you can easily make corrections every time and get better at it.

The correct pronunciation is a precondition

Pronunciation has a key role in successful communication both productively and receptively. English lessons should also focus on the teaching of pronunciation. A study carried out by Rajadurai (2001) on the attitude and concern for accurate English pronunciation among a group of Malaysian ESL teacher trainees showed that more than 80% of the trainees agreed that pronunciation is an important element in spoken English. You feel more confident to speak English if you can pronounce it well. You would love to sound like a native speaker. An ability to pronounce English words correctly is a significant achievement. One's proficiency in English may be perceived as 'good' if he or she can pronounce it well. Those with good pronunciation can get good jobs in the future. Good pronunciation reflects high proficiency in language use. If your pronunciation is improper, other people may have trouble understanding you even if you express your ideas logically and coherently.

How to Improve your English pronunciation?

There are 5 techniques by which you can improve your pronunciation.

1. The inspection technique

- Play an audio/ video recording of an English speaker
- Listen to the first sentence and record yourself saying the same words. (The imitation technique- Chapter 14)
- After you have recorded your video compare your recorded sentence with the original speaker
- Listen closely and try to sound like the speaker

This is a simple yet powerful tool. Only after a few sentences, you will find some habitual mistakes in your pronunciation. Once you become aware of these things, it should not be difficult to imitate the correct pronunciation with 100% accuracy. This method is very effective for two reasons:

- Spotting your mistakes on a recording is much easier than trying to do so while speaking and
- The power of comparison- when you do a side-by-side comparison between your and the speaker's pronunciation, it gives you a crystal-clear idea that where you need to improve.

2. The shadowing technique

We have already discussed the Shadowing technique in chapter 16. When you are copying the original speakers, imitating the original speakers then you are improving your pronunciation side by side.

3. Emphasize phrases

When the speaker speaks in English you can notice stress and unstressed phrases. You need to notice when the speaker goes up and when he goes down. When the speaker is emphasizing certain phrases, he is pushing words that are longer and he is louder. It's like going up on a hill with those emphasized phrases. Notice that pattern of stress or unstress. The pronunciation of the word may differ from the actual dictionary pronunciation. When you are stressing that word, you want to make a point or maybe you want the audience to focus on that particular idea.

5. Emphasizing within words

This is called syllable stress. Every word in English has one syllable that is stressed more than others. Let me tell you, what do we mean by syllables and what do you mean by syllable stress. Understand that pronouncing the word properly relates to syllable stress. This means if you know which syllable to stress in the word, you are going to be able to pronounce that word perfectly.

What is a syllable? Every word has one/ two/ three or maybe even 10 parts depending upon the length of the word. Every part of the word is called a syllable. However, the question is how do I know how many syllables are there or how many parts are there in a particular word?

Let's try this simple exercise. Put your hand under your chin and watch. Now let me check how many times my chin drops when I say my name, which is obviously a word. SU-RA-BHI. My chin is dropping three times, the word has three syllables. When I say Surabhi, I am stressing the last syllable, right? That is called syllable stress.

To add on, in nouns and verbs syllable stress changes, which in turn changes the pronunciation this can be better understood by the words that are **called 'HETERONYMS'**. The HETERONYMS are the words that can have the exactly same spelling but have different pronunciations and different meanings. For example:

Desert (noun- a place which is dry and Barren)- **DE**+SERT

Desert (verb- to abandon/ leave alone)- DE+**SERT**

5. Practice with minimal pairs

The list of minimal pairs is the perfect way to practice English pronunciation because students have to distinguish between two similar sounds.

What are minimal pairs?These are two similar sounding words that have only one phonological element different and they have different meanings and spellings too. These words help in improving your pronunciation by making your speech clear.

Some words are different in only one phonetic sound. So, when you practice speaking these words regularly, your tongue gets accustomed to using different phonological sounds. For instance:

Grammar; glamour

Royal; Loyal

Light; Right

Belly; Berry

Bloom; Groom

Climb; Crime

Sick; Thick

Song; Thong

Force; Fourth

Myth; Miss

There are many more to be found on the internet. As you practice these your English pronunciation is going to improve immensely.

English speaking is an inevitable part of our lives. But we need to understand that there is a difference between speaking and speaking effectively. There is a difference between talking and talking sense. So, it is essential to work on your communication skills while you are on your English learning journey.

CHAPTER TWENTY-ONE

Be Relentless- Stay Confident

"I can speak quite fearlessly, without any inhibitions in my practices or with my patients. But as soon as I face my seniors or my colleagues who are fluent English speakers, I get nervous and I retreat to my native language."- says Dr. Anya Misra (a psychologist), one of my students.

This problem is also faced by most of the non-native speakers. When they have to speak with native speakers, they get frozen, they get petrified, and nervous. They forget the words; they forget the sentences and they don't remember what they wanted to speak.

This is an unavoidable situation. Because if you wish to improve your English communication, you have to communicate with native speakers and fluent English speakers.

Speaking with confidence is one way to speak fluently. Confidence can drastically help you to enhance your English-speaking skills. When your nervousness is an obvious emotional feeling inside, how you can sound confident? In this chapter let us understand how to tackle this fearful situation.

How to Stay Confident?

In the previous chapters, we discussed that English learning is 80% mindset (psychology) and 20% English habits. So, you need to have a correct mindset not only while learning English but speaking English as well.

1. Don't be too embarrassed to speak

The most important way you will improve your English is by speaking and I mean speaking a great deal. You can possibly improve with practice. if you feel excessively embarrassed or humiliated and you keep on analyzing all the time, you won't improve on speaking in English. If you feel too embarrassed and ashamed, you really will not advance as fast as you could.

Your brain is the most powerful and the most stupid part of your body. If you let yourself know you can't talk in English, your brain will begin to trust you. So, it truly will hamper your progress. That implies, that u will not have the option to advance further and you will begin to accept what you are telling yourself. So, the way that you will improve is by practicing and what I suggest you do is 3 ways of practicing.

"Little Skittle"

Now by this I mean doing little things, that will assist you with working on your English speaking and gaining confidence. For instance, imagine you are going out, you are going to a place where you realize they communicate in English. You could order your food in English in such a place. This way it's something modest yet you are giving yourself that chance to rehearse your English and to grow your self-esteem.

Record Yourself

Simultaneously another incredible tip is if you don't have anybody to speak in English with or a to practice communication in English however you can record yourself, speaking in English. This is an extraordinary way to develop your confidence in English speaking and to practice and you can listen to yourself several times too. So you can improve on any mistakes that you have made and afterward you can work on those too.

Mirror Talk

Another way you can do this is by talking in the mirror. It might sound somewhat bizarre or feel somewhat amusing from the beginning yet it's an extraordinary way again to rehearse your speaking

So, either recording or talking with yourself in the mirror is giving yourself those positive affirmations and truly constructing your confidence could bring a sea change in your levels.

2. Don't feel sorry for your standard

Don't apologize for your standard of English and this is a really significant one because people are least bothered about your errors when talking in English, the truth is they would appreciate your thoughts & ideas. In case you are apologizing for your level you are not, giving the individual you are addressing, an opportunity to your thoughts. They just do not pay attention to your suggestions and they start making guesses about your level and that is something that you really don't want them to do. You don't want them to assume your degree of communication in English.

Learning a language is a challenge and the way that you have taken on the test and that you are rehearsing and attempting to learn English is commendable and ought to be appreciated. So, you ought to be a lot kinder to yourself and just do whatever it takes not to apologize for your level. Since you have supposedly made considerable progress in your learning journey, recall how far you have come along in your journey and what you have done to arrive here. You should have faced a lot of difficulties to get to the level where you are right now. And you are still advancing. So be glad for that and don't apologize for level.

What you could do at any point is perhaps, mention to the individual that you are learning English and you're genuinely trying. Telling that you are learning, shows that you are somewhat vulnerable. They may then really attempt to help you rather than thinking you aren't entirely perfect at speaking in English. They may offer you a compliment or appreciation for trying. This is greatly important because when you are honest with the people, they will see the value in your genuineness. And what's more, you have the chance to practice your English speaking instead of saying sorry for your level. So, remember that don't apologize for your standard.

3. Don't be scared to make Mistakes

Don't be afraid to commit errors in English. Mistakes are a piece of learning and you realize committing mistakes is an incredible method for learning. When I look back upon my language learning, the occasions that I have committed errors, are the occasions that I reflect on the most and they are the things that I will quite often remember all the more. So, you can commit tons of errors when you are communicating in English. Since it's an extraordinary method for learning.

People will not judge you for using terrible grammar. Honestly, they truly don't care about your grammar they are more concerned about your knowledge experience ideas, and suggestions. They are glad that you genuinely trying to connect with them and have a discussion. They are not bothered by how you are speaking they are more inspired by the meaning of what you are saying, they are keener about what you are trying to tell them. So remember that it's not about speaking accurately, it is about interacting with people, trying to have a discussion, trying to get them to understand what you are willing to say, and that way you can begin to build relationships with people.

At the beginning of your English journey, it is more important to work on speaking than learning Grammar. When you will ultimately begin to speak, you will always be thinking about the Grammar far too much and also about the mistakes that you are making and it will likely slow your progress. It may cause you to lose your confidence. Whereas, if you begin with speaking and when you have a fundamental level, you begin to learn grammar. You will observe the real practice significantly better and you can develop your confidence more.

Realize that fluent English speakers & natives commit errors too. Don't assume that they speak perfectly. I can't explain to you the number of times I have been speaking to someone and they make several errors all the time just because when they are speaking naturally. So even they make mistakes and even you should not stop yourself from speaking due to the fear of mistakes.

4. Don't get disappointed

Don't get baffled with yourself assuming you are talking in poor slow and broken English. When you get disappointed with yourself, you quite obstruct your brain. Your brain will be blocked. You will be centered around your dissatisfactions and resentments. This will not only kill your desire to talk, but it will also diminish the importance of what you want to say.

Instead of having these negative feelings try to be innovative. Utilize your expressions, emotions, gestures, or even props to get your idea across. This is a much better method for communication than surrendering or getting discontented and furious with yourself. You can advance in your learning and gain confidence, even from what you are doing in those moments of dissatisfaction. I understand it's difficult. I've experienced this, many times. Just try to stay calm and take a full deep breath and recollect your thoughts and simply try and think of an alternate approach to make your point. Take as much time as you want and like I said before try to be creative with your explanations. I am sure you'll be able to get across it.

The KEY is to is to interpret your anxiety as energy, your nervousness as excitement. Author Simon Sinek has an extraordinary approach to this. In one of his talks where he states watching the London Olympics, he states that he was annoyed by the way all the journalists asked all the athletes the same stupid question, "Are you nervous?" or "Were you nervous?". Whether it was before or after the event. And every single time all the athletes gave the exact same answer, "No I was excited." or "No I am excited." These elite athletes had learned to interpret body stimulus for nervousness into a stimulus for excitement. They had learned to interpret what their body was telling them not as nervousness but as excitement. He explains how you can take up any business and transform it into a fervor to make incredible outcomes and progress.

So, you could do the same with English. Rather than continually doubting yourself, "Oh, I am so anxious to talk in English!" or "I am so confused at this time", you should instantly be able to let yourself know that you are excited. It becomes even better if you know the reason "Why?". This is an extraordinary method of reconstructing your thoughts so that as opposed to feeling super anxious at that time you are energized at the chance to learn or to talk in English or to have a discussion with somebody or advance in your learning. So, the next time, whenever you are out or you need to attempt to talk in English train your mind not to be anxious and in a split second be energized.

5. Don't let it affect you emotionally

Don't let it affect you emotionally when people don't understand you. This is easier said than done. But this has happened to me too, when I made mistakes, I have had remarks from people that are so focused on correcting my mistakes and grammar that they are least bothered with the content I am sharing. People find all sorts of pleasure in finding faults with people. It is human nature, so let it be. What you need to do is just focus on your thoughts and try speaking as clearly as possible focusing on your pronunciation too. In this way, the person you are speaking with has the most obvious opportunity to understand what you are trying to say. and you will not get annoyed and you will not think about it personally in case they are not exactly understanding you. However, the best part is you are still taking the responsibility and trying to speak clearly, and concentrating on that.

6. Don't compare

Don't compare yourself with other language learners. Each person is an individual. Everybody has an extremely special journey; it can be on their language learning or other different things in life. So it's important not to compare yourself with others since you don't have a clue what their journey has been so far, you don't have the foggiest idea how long they have been learning English, and you don't know what they have done to get to the level they are at. Learning a language is a challenge. So, you should be glad for where you are in your journey at the present moment. Be glad for what you have accomplished so far. Don't compare yourself with others and begin to feel frustrated about it. Consider how far you exclusively have come on your journey and utilize that inspiration to continue moving forward, to continue progressing, and to continue to fight any obstructions that you face.

Now, suppose you experience somebody that has a further developed level, you have. He speaks better English. Would you be able to utilize that as an inspiration to work more enthusiastically and track down various methods of learning that will help you with your progress and get to that level? Or, would you crib, comparing yourself with him and getting frustrated?

Additionally, remember that everybody has an alternate strength and others will have different qualities from you and perhaps language learning is one of the most challenging and demanding of all. In any phase of language learning be it in elementary, high school, or University, you will meet people with various levels and strengths. You will meet people that can do dozens of various things and are at a level that might be far superior to you. Yet there are few things which you can do better than them, find that something that and feel proud of yourself. So, remember that everybody is different, everybody's journey is different. You should be glad for yours. You should feel motivated by that and use it as an inspiration to advance and take motivation from others rather than looking at yourself and getting disappointed by it.

7. Don't feel contented

If you think you are fluent enough, don't get too presumptuous or arrogant. Remember spoken English is a skill, it's an art that needs to be practiced & polished regularly. It's bad to think in any case, that I've learned English, I don't have to practice any longer or I don't have to speak it any longer. This will harm your English speaking.

Remember that life is a journey and not a destination, so you never arrive at your destination with English language learning regardless of the level where you are. You still need to practice. Being arrogant can also make you lazy which is never something good, your English will deteriorate. Remember, **"If you don't use it, you lose it".**

Make sure to continue to practice whether it's little pockets of time every day or in some cases in the week. Continue to advance. You could even give a target to yourself as a part of fluency in English so that you don't stop moving ahead. Understand, it's a journey, regardless of where you are in your journey there will always be one more level. For instance, in English, even if you are an advanced speaker, still you may not have the foggiest idea about each of the words in the English language. So, there may be times when you are sitting in front of the TV and u need to pay special attention to a word since it's something that you haven't heard previously. So, remember it's a journey and there is always a next level that you can reach.

CHAPTER TWENTY-TWO

DEVELOPING TENACITY- THE ENGLISH HABITS

"You cannot change your future, but you can change your habits; and surely your habits will change your future."

- Dr. A. P. J. Abdul Kalam

You wake up in the morning, all set to start your day early with your English practice, but your mind makes you press that snooze button. You decide that you are going to move forward on your journey to be a fluent speaker, but your mind makes you break that promise. Afterward, all that you feel is guilty about it.

The fact is, the moment you commit to yourself, I am going to listen to English Podcasts, I am going to practice imitation and shadowing, several times, no matter what, your brain is triggered in the opposite direction. A part of your mind is always looking for instant gratification. It's always looking for a short-term win. It's the part of us that complains, cribs, cries, compares, and criticizes. But here is the other part of the brain which is focused on the 'root cause'. It is focused on discipline and long-term gain which is excellence in English speaking skills. This part of the brain is calm composed, collaborative, caring, and compassionate. There is a constant argument between the two parts of the brain. One wants you to get back to sleep and relax. The other wants you to practice proactively. If there is anything that will help you achieve your dreams, it is your habits.

The thing which plays the role of the referee here is your HABITS. Your habits create a barrier between the two parts of the brain and help your mind take the right decisions. It's rightly said, "First you make the habits and then the habits make you." If you want to speak English fluently, confidently, powerfully, subconsciously, effortlessly, and naturally, then you have to work on your habits.

H- Have a powerful 'Why'

You need a really powerful reason for 'why you want to learn English?' and become a fluent and confident English speaker. If you don't have a deep profound reason, it will be really difficult. For instance, if someone says, "I want to quit smoking just because I want to do it." It's different from someone saying, "I want to quit smoking because I love my family. I want to save my family. I want to keep my family together. This habit is ruining my family time. So I really want to kick this habit out of my life." The contrast in the reason is all that makes the difference. We have discussed, how to discover "your powerful Why" in chapter 12. To develop habits, you must have a goal in life, a purpose to live, and a reason to get up in the morning. Your goal must be to excel in English. Ask yourself, what is that big, deep reason to enhance my English? Having a strong why is what builds the foundation of your habits.

A- Awareness

Your awareness gives more information, knowledge, depth, and power to your WHY. This means you may submit yourself to a mentor or a coach, who guides you through. You may speak to people who have already mastered the habit of English practice, who have made English a part of their daily life. You may focus on reading books, listening to podcasts, or watching the videos in English. The more you absorb Information, the sooner will be the transformation. The awareness, the information, and the knowledge are consistently going to strengthen your WHY.

Every time you think of deviating from your goal, your mind will remind you of your mentor. Every time you want to relax your mind will remind you of the person you spoke to and you will want to achieve a similar kind of mastery in English. When you want to create a habit change in your life make sure what you listen to, what you read, and what you speak about is about English only. When you immerse yourself in that way you will see an immense impact on your life.

B- Be Consistent

You have to consistently make English the priority of your life. If you are not able to do so, it's just not going to happen. You have to repeat the actions, and the practice lessons and you have to prioritize around them. If you really want to make something a priority in your life, it has to be a small step and a big priority. Often, we try to bring a big change in our lives by changing every area of our life, and then naturally nothing changes. The better idea is to choose one area and make it your top priority. So, if you want to practice your English lessons make them your top priority for that day. Set an easily manageable time. What you think or say the whole day, is not important. Your actions are important. 'What you DO'- is all that matters. The bridge between where you are and where you want to go is called habits.

Habits need repetitions. It is a must to repeat it every single day. The question is not whether you like it or not. The question is whether it is important or not. The price which you need to pay to develop these habits is "self-discipline." Repeating your habits even when you don't like them is self-discipline. Most people do it when they feel like doing it. But there are few, who do it even when they don't feel like doing it. This is what sets apart the achievers from the average. Stop TV, open a book, stop water-cooler gossiping, get to discussions, stop surfing the social media, start influencing, stop binge-watching and start investing in courses for improving yourselves. Start working on your English-speaking skills and start working on your vocabulary on your confidence.

I-Incorporate

When you do it with someone, you feel that you are growing with someone. That's why form a community or join a tribe or a group of people that are trying to aim for natural subconscious effortless English speaking. With a community of like-minded people, you are more likely to achieve that. You can join my Facebook community-Fearless Communicators Tribe, where you will find so many people to motivate you every day. Motivation will get you started, but it's the habits that will keep you going. Responsibility and accountability make you more likely to get to your destination.

T- Track your growth

Make sure you recognize what amazing growth you are making. Take a moment to say, "look how far I've come." Because our mind again tricks us and always makes us realize how far we have to go. The bridge between where you are and where you want to go is called habits. So, it's important to track how much you've grown. Remind yourself of the difference you've made.

English Habits

Learning English or learning any language takes time and effort and dedication. But the most successful non-native English speakers, have found a way for English to become a part of their daily life. **It has become a habit just like brushing your teeth.** It is an automatic behavior. You get up in the morning and just brush your teeth. No matter where you are, whatever may be the setup. Whether you are at your friend's house, on a train, or traveling. The first thing you do after waking is brush your teeth. So it is a ritual that you follow religiously. If you wish to improve, your English practice should become a daily ritual.

There are a few things that you can and you should be doing every day to improve your English and you must do all of these, every day. They're not humongous tasks and you can fit them into your daily routine with ease.

1. Pronunciation- Practice

The very first thing is that you should be practicing your pronunciation every day. It doesn't mean, trying to get rid of your accent completely but making it clear enough to be understood by others comfortably, whenever you speak in English.

Several advanced English learners have amazing grammar and vocabulary skills but face so much trouble communicating because their accent makes it quite challenging for the listener to understand them. For sure, pronunciation affects smooth, positive, comfortable, and effective conversation.

It is quite possible while you were learning English, your teacher might not have paid much attention to pronunciation. They may not have prioritized it at that time. You see, if you learned English at school, it's quite possible, the main aim was probably to get high scores in your exam. Pronunciation was probably not your priority at that time but in the real world when you're using English to speak with other people, your pronunciation, your fluency when you speak, it's so incredibly important.

Building the habit of learning and practicing using the correct pronunciation is going to save you lots of stress and confusion down the line. Consistent practice of pronunciation every day will help you to make noticeable improvements in a short span of time.

Chapter 20, talks about all the possible convenient ways of practicing and improving your pronunciation. Every day repetitions will help your mouth muscles to get accustomed to creating English sounds and get more comfortable doing it. Just five or ten minutes of practice a day is more than enough. Just remember consistency is the key

2. Soak your brain in English

When you soak your brain in English it develops grammar naturally. You speak grammatically correct English but without studying the grammar rules. Create, at least one opportunity to absorb English every day. Allow your brain to absorb information like a sponge, soaking things up. Absorbing new ideas, new words, and new ways of expressing yourself. You can do this in lots of different ways.

Reading

We have discussed a lot about Reading as a source of learning English in chapter 19. Fluent English speakers have developed the habit of reading. They read a lot. They read whatever they can lay their hands on, books, magazines, newspapers, and blog posts. They just read. They use only English as a language for input. As a result of this, they acquire and develop grammar and vocabulary naturally and subconsciously.

Listening

The fluent and confident English speakers listen to a lot of English content. They listen to easy and understandable English. They listen to the English they want to use while speaking and writing. You must listen regularly and repetitively. You can listen to a podcast or an audiobook. (Ref. Chapter 14)

Watching

Non-native fluent speakers watch English movies or any other videos on YouTube. They select the language English only, not their native language. When you are watching a video, you are using two senses. You see the picture through the eyes and you listen to the audio through the ears. When you are using two senses the absorption of the English is more. You acquire and develop grammar naturally and quickly. This is a very powerful and effective way.

You can probably mix up these activities during the week, to keep things interesting. For example, a podcast on Monday. Reading a book on Tuesday. Whatever suits you.

Now again, this isn't a hugely time-consuming task but it's worth spending some time searching for the right type of content. It must be something that interests you and excites you because you need to look forward to doing it every single day. It shouldn't feel like you're doing English practice.

3. Write to keep your memory bright.

Writing every day has its own benefits. By writing I don't mean writing an essay. It's just about writing a few thoughts or a few ideas, which are just for you. Nobody ever has to see it.

It helps your vocabulary to stick. Writing is one of the best ways to remember and recall new words, phrases, idioms, and expressions that you've come across, while reading, listening, or watching English content.

As you're reading or watching TV shows or books, you come across new ideas and words, you must write them down. Gradually, start to use them yourself. Think of sentences and your own ideas about how to use these words. By producing your own sentences rather than just listening to other people's, it just gets embedded in your mind.

4. Speaking

One interesting habit that non-native fluent speakers have is that they speak in English. Even though they are not fluent in English initially they start speaking in English. Although, they speak in broken English, eventually, they develop the flow. This development comes through all the above habits. The combination of all the above activities along with speaking helps them speak English subconsciously and naturally.

You must join English discussions about topics that interest you. Be a part of an active group or an online community, for example, my community- Fearless Communicators Tribe, where people interact. Where they share their ideas, they give opinions and you'll be able to respond. So, you may comment and enjoy being a part of the discussion as it happens. That makes it easier to develop a daily habit because you simply need to check and see what everyone else has been talking about and give your opinion.

Your English habits will decide your English communication and fluency and that will decide your status, your income, and your success. If you want a good job, respect, relationships, financial independence, and good public speaking skills, then English habits are the only way you can achieve it.

Remember, good habits take longer to develop and stay. It's not as simple as deciding you're going to do it. Good habits are like the crops, you have to sow the seeds water them nurture them take care of them like a baby. Whereas bad habits are like weeds, you don't do anything but they will grow. That is the reason why it is difficult to develop good habits. You have to choose between life-changing habits or life-destroying habits. Life is all about the choices you make every single day. See a big change in your English communication and your entire life, by changing your habits. Because it's all about your habits.

CHAPTER TWENTY-THREE

Strategy to success-The Turbo English Mastery Program

"A goal without an action plan is a daydream"

- Nathaniel Branden

So, you've almost completed the book. You know the core Turbo English Mastery System. You understand the methods to help you learn English subconsciously, naturally, and speak fluently and automatically with confidence. I have proved why traditional methods don't work. "In theory, practice and theory are same, but in practice they are different." I have walked you through the latest research and my personal experience from the past 8 years of teaching the English language to hundreds of students from different spheres of life. I have tried my best to motivate you that English is made for you. You are not bad at English. you are not a bad English learner. It's just that you have not been taught using the natural way, the subconscious way.

The only cure for poor English-speaking skills is not to study and memorize concepts and rules. The cure is much easier and even simpler to apply, it is to follow "The Secret Psychology of Learn English – The Subconscious Way." When you apply the correct psychology and learn English the subconscious way, you no longer need to study the boring textbooks and go through the tedious grammar drills. All you need to do is follow the simple techniques, used in the Turbo English Mastery Program.

1. Reprogram your brain by changing your limiting beliefs to empowering beliefs.
2. Control your Emotions by Reprogramming the Anchors.
3. Set big deep and strong goals
4. Be energetic and keep moving
5. Learn using your ears not your eyes. Listening is the key to language proficiency.
6. Utilize the power of phrases.
7. Invest your time and energy in repetition. Repetition is the secret of non-native fluent speakers.
8. Learn grammar subconsciously and naturally through grammar stories.
9. Learn real English by using only authentic English materials as done by the natives.
10. Reading is vital for English mastery.

The Turbo English Mastery system is the perfect way to help you reach your destination- fluency in English. But as we discussed earlier, even the best vehicles fail if they run on poor fuel. The secret psychology- your empowering beliefs, your positive emotions, your energized body movements, your motivated attitude, and your big strong goals, add the correct fuel to the engine of English learning. You need to speak with full confidence. Just believe in the methodology and yourself.

Why Take action?

So, you have understood the concepts. But is that enough to make you a fluent and natural English speaker? Imagine learning how to drive a car by just reading a book. Or playing guitar by just watching a video lesson. Is it possible? Probably not. The truth is that you have to physically sit behind the steering, and put your feet on the accelerator to move the car. The truth is that you actually need to run your fingers on those strings to play fine music, to make those melodious tunes. Similarly, just reading this book, no matter how many times, no matter how deeply, is not going to take you too far on your journey to fluency. What is the use of knowing all the techniques, if you haven't utilized them if you haven't tried them out yet?

It's time to take action. It is important to know the correct line of action and follow the right direction. However, change can be brought only with your actions. The decision to act will bring the transformation you want. If you just keep learning and don't put them into action that means you are procrastinating. And procrastination and success share a very deep and strong bond. They are the best of enemies.

After reading this book you must be feeling really motivated and inspired, by all the techniques shared by me. But what change it will bring in your life if you don't use those techniques to take real and tangible actions. Just reading this book won't magically transform you into a confident and natural speaker. For that, you need to take action and apply all those techniques in your life. Actions carve out success.

Success is a journey, not a destination. We need to keep on moving, keep on pushing our limits. We can't just make one single attempt and wait for the change to happen. Taking action one day might be easy. But doing it every day regularly and changing it into a habit is a challenge. Once the habit is formed, it becomes a power that no one can take away from you. It is an invincible weapon that will help you face all the resistance in your way. Actions transform into habits, and habits lead to success. The more you repeat the new actions, the more natural you become at it.

Taking the first step is crucial because if you never start it will never become a habit. Pablo Picasso once said, "Action is the foundational key to all success." Just learning or reading wouldn't bring any change. The best course of action is to take an action. So, stop procrastinating and remove the resistance. Take an Action Now!

The plan of Action

So, are you ready to speak English automatically and naturally? Are you ready to experience the feeling of confidence and ease every time you speak in English? Are you willing to give up your grammar books, vocabulary lists, and communication worksheets? Are you ready to experience the joy of learning English? Are you willing to focus on communication with real people? Are you ready to fulfill your big dreams?

How to do that? How to design a day which should inculcate all that I have discussed in the book? How to follow the English Habits? (Chapter-22). Because that is what you need, good **subconscious habits.** So that you use correct English without ever thinking about it at all. What would a typical day with Turbo English Mastery Program look like?

1. Waking up in the Morning

Play on your favorite energizing music, and review your list of positive English experiences and empowering beliefs. As you read each point on the list keep on remembering the emotion of a positive experience. Think about your big strong goal- how is English going to help you achieve it. Let the music play, jump, smile, or even dance a bit until you feel energetic and elevated. Immediately play an easy and interesting English podcast or an audiobook. You can also play a lesson or a grammar story from the Turbo English Mastery Program. Start listening to it. As you listen and imitate don't let your smile fade away. Keep moving, keep walking. Don't sit down and relax. Keep following the imitation or shadowing, shouting out loudly. The moment you feel your energy dropping, play the music again.

This morning ritual is not going to take more than 30 minutes of yours. It's an amazing way to start your day by improving your English.

2. Traveling to work.

While you are traveling to work or school or college, listen to more English content. At this time, you may quietly listen with your headphones plugged in as there may be people around.

3. At lunch

You can use this free time to listen to more English. If you may find a space, if possible, you can even shout out doing shadowing and imitation of the audio lesson or the grammar story.

4. Returning home.

This time can be utilized for quietly listening again. You may repeat or continue the same audiobook as you were listening to in the morning.

5. At home

Before going to bed, listen to more English. Play the energizing music, create a high emotional state, listen to the grammar story, and if possible, shout out following shadowing or imitation, imitate all the emotions, or even exaggerate. For best results do this at the same time every night. This would cost another 30 minutes.

You may also practice using the movies or Netflix, chapter 14. You can also do the 3-day vocabulary practice, chapter 15. You may also read a book.

Keep listening to English, even if you are waiting at the doctor's or standing in a queue. Let English play in the background if you are cooking, washing, or doing other chores. You may take fifteen minutes from the time you usually spend reading a newspaper. If by chance you miss a couple of days, you need not worry about getting behind with the course. For if you devote approximately an hour in an evening to the work, you'll easily catch up on the whole week's exercises. Keep yourself submerged in English throughout the day.

By following this daily routine as a ritual and creating small time pockets for your learning process, you are creating strong habits. The next step is repetition. Repeat the same routine every day. Repeat the same audios for deeper and more intense absorption of the language. Listen to the same grammar story, same audiobook, same podcast. Watch the same movie scene. Repeat the same things for the entire week or more and try to master each audio before moving to the next.

The secret inner voice

The main principle of the Turbo English Mastery Program is habit-forming. You'll be able to speak fluent and natural English by constantly using the right forms. But how are you to understand in each case what's correct? You develop "The sense of correctness" which solves this problem in a simple, unique, sensible way.

Whenever you mispronounce a word or whenever you violate correct grammatical usage or use the incorrect word to precise what you meant, you'll hear your inner voice say gently, "That's wrong, it should be thus-and-so."

It would not be long before you'd subconsciously use the right form and therefore the right words in speaking. If you continued to form an equivalent mistake, each time, patiently, your inner voice would help you realize what was right. You would be your own mentor who wouldn't tease or humiliate you, but on the contrary, would support and assist you. In a few months, you'd automatically speak and write correct English.

This is the correct psychology to learn English. All you need is to follow the techniques and form a habit. It's the repetition of the same lessons over and over until you start using them without thought. So, if you continually use the correct forms of speech, again and again, the habit of correct speech becomes ingrained.

When you know just where your danger spots are, you can easily make yourself safe against them. The Turbo English Mastery course does exactly this thing for you. It's the silent voice behind you, whispering to you whenever you committed a mistake, guiding you to develop fluent English, with the "sense of correctness".

The best thing about the audio lessons in the Turbo English Mastery Program is that you can do the activity from anywhere. You can be on the foot and keep listening at the same time. Follow this intensive schedule with tenacity for at least six months in order to see tangent results. Although English learning is a gradual and consistent process. It takes time to develop mastery. Still, you will be able to see results in these six months. In the beginning, nothing may seem to happen with your speaking. Though you start understanding more English, speaking may seem no different. Suddenly after a few months, something amazing will happen. English phrases and words begin to flow out automatically and subconsciously. It begins with a few at first, then more and more with every passing week. By the time you reach the end of six months, you will find a noticeable improvement in your speaking.

This improvement comes around with the consistent English Habits and routine. This consistency is the secret to your success. You may not start speaking perfectly, even the native speakers do not speak perfectly. But you will develop confidence and ease with English. "Consistency is what transforms average to excellence."

You have been using the old traditional methods for years. Did they help? Are you able to speak English naturally and fluently? Trust the Turbo English Mastery System for at least six months.

But you need to follow the system with full devotion. The improvements you achieve by the end of six months are going to amaze you.

You will finally achieve what you have been waiting for. You will see yourself improve. You will observe yourself acquiring this powerful language. You start instantly to put into use everything you have learned. The more you use it, the deeper become your good English habits. Words and phrases will flow automatically; pronunciation will become clear effortlessly, and the grammar will improve subconsciously. The feeling of confidence will surface naturally.

From the social point of view, you'll gain something that's so priceless that you simply can't fathom it. You'll gain that mark of honor that will continue as long as you exist, and which nobody can ever take from you. You'll gain fluency in speech that will establish you as an informed and knowledgeable person in whatever society you explore. You'll gain the self-confidence and self-respect that English inspires.

You will have the key to creating people such as you. You will be able to share your knowledge, learnings, and experiences with the world. Everyone will seek you out, magnetized by the new charm of your personality. You'll be ready to tell entertaining stories. Your quick and straightforward command of English will help you indulge in witty and clever conversations. And when serious subjects are being discussed, you'll be able to express your ideas clearly, forcefully, and with persuasion.

I want you to believe in yourself. I want you to understand that English is made for you. You will succeed on your journey to fluency. You will finally become a confident, fearless, powerful, and natural English speaker. Let the past be dead and buried. Just forget all your struggles with English. Let them go. Overcome your apprehensions, hesitation and inhibitions, fears, stress, and anxiety. Overcome your 'English Trauma'. Follow, **"The Secret Psychology of learning English- The Subconscious Way"**. Start afresh with a completely new system.

Wish you luck on your new journey to fluency.

Surabhi Jain
http://www.linkedin.com/in/surabhijain22
fearlesscommunication.in@gmail.com

Author's Bio

Surabhi Jain

Surabhi Jain is the founder-director of ***"The Turbo English Mastery"***program. She was born in the popular state of Uttar Pradesh located in North India. She is an entrepreneur, an educator, an IELTS trainer, a business communication coach, soft skills trainer, a Udemy course instructor, a writer, and a Language Acquisition Coach.

She believes language learning is a continuous process and calls herself a lifelong learner. With Hindi as her native language since childhood, she faced challenges with English speaking. She loves to research and explore various techniques and theories of English language learning and get connected with people who have learned English as a second language.

She finds extreme pleasure in teaching English and knowledge sharing. Since 1995, she has been training people from various walks of life, in English speaking and communication skills. She is a B. Com graduate.

She loves speaking. She has got an opportunity to speak on various prestigious platforms and has won several accolades as a public speaker.

She loves to share her stories, communicate with people, and know about their stories too.

Her book ***"The Secret Psychology of Learning English- The Subconscious Way"*** will be a game-changer for all the people who are still struggling to speak this language naturally and fluently with confidence, despite spending their time, money, and energy on learning this skill.

References

[1] Shawn L., Shaofeng Li, Fei Fei, Amy Thompson, Kimi Nakatsukasa, Seongmee Ahn, Xiao Quing Chen, Second Language Learners' Beliefs About Grammar Instruction and Error Correction, The Modern Language Journal, Volume 93, Issue 1, Spring 2009, pages 91-104.

[2] P. T. Rankin, The Importance of Listening Ability. The English Journal, 17(8), pp. 623–630, 1928.

[3] Md. Enamul Hoque, An Introduction to the Second Language Acquisition, In book: Language Acquisition, pp.1-23, Publisher: EDRC, Dhaka, Bangladesh, The Journal of EFL Education and Research, 2017.

[4] Ngar-Fun Liu, William Littlewood, Why do many students appear reluctant to participate in classroom learning discourse? System, vol. 25, Issue 3, pp. 371-384, ISSN 0346-251X, 1997.

[5] Miralpeix, Imma and Muñoz, Carmen, Receptive vocabulary size and its relationship to EFL language skills, International Review of Applied Linguistics in Language Teaching, vol. 56, no. 1, pp. 1-24, 2018.

[6] Celce-Murcia, M., Grammar Pedagogy in Second and Foreign Language Teaching. TESOL Quarterly, Vol. 25(3), pp. 459–480, 1991.

[7] Macaro, E., & Masterman, L., Does intensive explicit grammar instruction make all the difference? Language Teaching Research, 10(3), 297–327. 2006.

[8] Torky, Shaimaa Abd EL Fattah, The Effectiveness of a Task-Based Instruction Program in Developing the English Language Speaking Skills of Secondary Stage Students, Ph.D. Dissertation, Ain Shams University, 2006.

[9] Heller, Monica, Language, Skill and Authenticity in the Globalized New Economy, Noves SL.: Revista de sociolingüística, ISSN 1695-3711, no. 2, 2005.

[10] Sörqvist Patrik, Dahlström Örjan, Karlsson Thomas, Rönnberg Jerker, Concentration: The Neural Underpinnings of How Cognitive Load Shields Against Distraction , Frontiers in Human Neuroscience, vol. 10, 2016.

[11] Cook, Vivian J., Chomsky's Universal Grammar and Second Language Learning, Applied Linguistics Vol. 6 (1), pp. 2-18. 1985.

[12] Noam Siegelman, Inbal Arnon, The advantage of starting big: Learning from unsegmented input facilitates mastery of grammatical gender in an artificial language, Journal of Memory and Language, vol. 85, pp. 60-75, ISSN 0749-596X, 2005.

[13] Babita Tyagi, Listening: An Important Skill and Its Various Aspects, The Criterion, An International Journal in English, ISSN 0976-8165 Issue 12, 2013.

[14] Brown, Steven, Slow Down! The Importance of Repetition, Planning, and Recycling in Language Teaching, Paper Presented at the Meeting of the Ohio Teachers of English to Speakers of Other Languages, 2000.

[15] F Genesee, Integrating Language and Content: Lessons from Immersion. UC Berkeley: Center for Research on Education, Diversity, and Excellence, 1994.

[16] Kachru, Braj., The power and politics of English. World Englishes, vol. 5 (2-3), pp. 121-140. 1986.

[17] Steinbeck, Reinhold Building Creative Competence in Globally Distributed Courses through Design Thinking. Comunicar, 19, pp. 27-35, 2011.

[18] Dewaele Jean-Marc, Chen Xinjie, Padilla Amado M., Lake J., The Flowering of Positive Psychology in Foreign Language Teaching and Acquisition Research, Frontiers in Psychology, vol. 10, 2019.

[19] Story, Amber L., Self-Esteem and Memory for Favourable and Unfavourable Personality Feedback, Personality and Social Psychology Bulletin 24, no. 1, pp. 51–64, 1998

[20] Gregory C.D. Young, Maryanne Martin, Processing of information about self by neurotics, The British Psychologica;

Society, vol. 20, Issue3, pp. 205-212.

[21] Vural, H. The Relationship of Personality Traits with English Speaking Anxiety. Research in Educational Policy and Management, 1(1), pp. 55-74, 2019.

[22] Adrian Furnham, Hua Chu Boo, A literature review of the anchoring effect, The Journal of Socio-Economics, vol 40, Issue 1, pp. 35-42, ISSN 1053-5357, 2011.

[23] Tal Shafir, Stephan F. Taylor, Anthony P. Atkinson, Scott A. Langenecker, Jon-Kar Zubieta, Emotion regulation through execution, observation, and imagery of emotional movements, Brain and Cognition, vol. 82, Issue 2, pp. 219-227, 2013.

[24] N Cao Thanh, The Differences between Spoken and Written Grammar in English, in Comparison with Vietnamese. GIST – Education and Learning Research Journal, (11), 138–153, 2015.

[26] Abdulrahman, Tryanti; Basalama, Nonny, Widodo, Mohammad Rizky, The Impact of Podcasts on EFL Students' Listening Comprehension, International Journal of Language Education, vol. 2, Issue-2, pp. 23-33, 2018.

[27] Yaren Ding, Text memorization and imitation: The practices of successful Chinese learners of English, System, vol. 35, Issue 2, pp. 271-280, ISSN 0346-251X, 2007.

[28]www.chieflearningofficer.com/2013/01/10/engage-passive-learners/

[29] Hsieh, Jasper Kun-Ting & Dong, Da & Wang, Li Yi., A preliminary study of applying shadowing technique to English intonation instruction. Taiwan Journal of Linguistics. vol. 11. Pp. 43-66, 2013.

[30] Kadota, S., Shadowing as a Practice in Second Language Acquisition: Connecting Inputs and Outputs (1st ed.). Routledge, 2019.

[31] Febrina, W., Authentic vs Non-Authentic Materials in Teaching English as a Foreign Language (EFL) in Indonesia: Which One Matters More? , 2017.

[32] Alzu'bi, Mohammad Akram, The Effects of an Extensive Reading Program on Improving English as Foreign Language Proficiency in University Level Education, English Language Teaching, vol. 7 (1) pp. 28-35, 2014.

[33] Radiological Society of North America. (2012, November 25). Reading, writing and playing games may help aging brains stay healthy. Science Daily. Retrieved June 15, 2022.

[34] Slamet Riyanto, Ag. Bambang Setiyadi, Budi Kadaryanto, The role of attitude to language learning in reading comprehension, vol. 4 (3), Riyanto, 2015.

[35] Yamashita, Junko, Effects of extensive reading on reading attitudes in a foreign language, Reading in a Foreign Language, vol. 25 (2).pp. 248-263. 2013.

[36] English could snowball on Net, By Ted Smalley Bowen, Technology Research News, November 21, 2001.

[37] Campione, Estelle & Vronis, Jean, A Large-Scale Multilingual Study of Silent Pause Duration, 2002.

[38] P. Hartwell, Grammar, Grammars, and the Teaching of Grammar. College English, 47(2), 105–127, 1985.

[39] Benalia Yamina, Investigating the Effects of Using Shadowing techniques to Engage Countryside Pupils to Learn English as a Foreign Language, Master Thesis, Mohamed Kheider University of Biskra, Faculty of Letters and Languages Department of Foreign Languages, 2020.

[40] Shiamaa Abd EL Fattah Torky, The Effectiveness of a Task-Based Instruction Program in Developing the English Language Speaking Skills of Secondary Stage Students, Ph.D. Thesis, Ain Shams University Women's college Curricula and Methods of teaching Department, 2006.

[41] Patricia K. Kuhl, A new view of language acquisition, in Proc. of the National Academy of Sciences, 97 (22) 11850-11857, 2000.

[42] Wang, Yongliang et al. Researching and Practicing Positive Psychology in Second/Foreign Language Learning and Teaching: The Past, Current Status and Future Directions. Frontiers in

psychology vol. 12 731721. 19 Aug. 2021, doi:10.3389/fpsyg.2021.731721

[43]Amy Jenkins,Guided Meditation in the English language Classroom, americanenglish.state.gov/english-teaching-forum, 2015

[44] Patricia A. Duff, Repetition in Foreign Language Interaction, Ch-6, from the book-Second and Foreign Language Learning Through Classroom Interaction, Edited by Joan Kelly Hall and Lorrie Stoops Verplaetse, Published by Routledge, Taylor and Francis Group, 2014.

[45] Pinos-Ortiz, Mónica & Orbe-Guaraca, Mariory, The effects of the TPRS Method on the Students' English Vocabulary Acquisition. Dominio de las Ciencias. 4. 264. 10.23857/dc.v4i3.809. 2018.

[46] David Alley, Denise Overfield, An Analysis of the Teaching Proficiency Through Reading and Storytelling (TPRS) Method, Dimension 2008: Languages for the Nation, pp-13-25, in Procc. of the 2008 Joint Conference of the Southern Conference on Language Teaching and the South Carolina Foreign Language Teachers' Association.

[47] Chang, Shih-Chuan, A Contrastive Study of Grammar Translation Method and Communicative Approach in Teaching English Grammar. English Language Teaching. 4. 10.5539/elt.v4n2p13, 2011.

[48] D. Renukadevi, The Role of Listening in Language Acquisition; the Challenges & Strategies in Teaching Listening. International Journal of Education and Information Studies, 4, 2277-3169. 2014.

Printed by Libri Plureos GmbH in Hamburg,
Germany